White Cane Religion

And Other Messages From the Brownsville Revival

White Cane Religion

And Other Messages From the Brownsville Revival

Stephen Hill

Revival Press

An Imprint of
Destiny Image® **Publishers, Inc.**
P.O. Box 310
Shippensburg, PA 17257-0310

ISBN 1-56043-186-5

For Worldwide Distribution
Printed in the U.S.A.

This book and all other Destiny Image, Revival Press, and Treasure House books are available at Christian bookstores and distributors worldwide.

For a U.S. bookstore nearest you, call **1-800-722-6774**. For more information on foreign distributors, call **717-532-3040**. Or reach us on the Internet: **http://www.reapernet.com**

Dedication

It is a fact that an evangelist often reaps where he has not sown. I would like to recognize the faithful ones who have sought God with petitions and intercessory cries over the souls of their loved ones. To you who have labored in prayer and sowed in tears, I humbly dedicate this manuscript.

Contents

Foreword

It is one of the tragedies of the contemporary Church in the West that the ministry of the evangelist has fallen into disrepute. For many, the evangelist is merely an entrepreneur, a slick, smooth-talking salesman who knows how to bring in the bucks. He is a showman, a performer, a professional. He dresses right, talks right, and exudes self-confidence. This is a picture of the modern evangelist, a far cry from the classic portrait of a brokenhearted soul winner who is stirred by the cries of a dying generation and is moved with compassion to reach the lost at any cost.

Steve Hill is an evangelist in the classic, best sense of the word, and it is one of the blessings of the Brownsville Revival that the ministry of the evangelist is being restored to the contemporary Church. Let me introduce you to the man and his message. (Actually, the man and the message are one; Steve *is* what he preaches.)

From an early age, Steve Hill made wrong choices, following the voice of evil instead of the voice of God. He became a narcotics addict, a serious drug dealer, a heavy drinker, and a criminal. Arrested 13 times, facing serious jail time, terribly oppressed by demonic powers, Steve was on the edge of destruction when a gospel minister reached out to him and told him of the love of God. He was instantly delivered and immediately wanted to tell everyone what Jesus had done for him. "He who is forgiven much loves much" (see Lk. 7:47). That was in 1975. Since then, he has preached around the world, especially in Spanish-speaking countries, spending seven years in Argentina in the midst of a great national revival. He has ministered to lawless gangs on the streets of America and to hardened kids in our nation's schools. Always there is one thing that moves him: *souls*. He is literally driven to see sinners saved.

I have listened to him preach night after night in the Brownsville Revival, and it is no small thing to say that through the piercing messages that he has delivered in the last 20 months, *more than 100,000 people have gotten right with God*. The messages have hit home! You are about to read some of them for yourself. Prepare to change!

Steve preaches with a heart on fire to spare people from a hell of fire. His soul burns today so that people will not burn tomorrow. He pleads and warns night after night, never ceasing or tiring, always searching for one more soul, always looking out for the confused down-and-outer, always going after that last straying sheep. Night after night you can only weep as you see hundreds of sinners, backsliders, religious hypocrites, Christians who have fallen, leaders who need to repent—the list is now 20 months long—flocking to the altar, often *running* to the altar, even *sprinting* to the altar to fully surrender their lives to God, to receive fresh cleansing, to make a brand-new start. And the fruit is lasting! Already, there are dramatic drops in the crime rate here in Escambia County (while juvenile crime in Florida rose 1 percent in 1996, it dropped 13 percent in Escambia County), the schools have been affected, the churches have been affected, the community has been affected. And while there is no doubt that prayer, worship, and holiness are the fuel that keeps the revival burning, and while it is clear that the "wood" for the fire is provided by the hundreds of thousands of hungry souls who have attended the revival services over the weeks, the match that ignites the flames afresh every night is the message delivered by Steve.

I have watched him preach through sickness, his voice half gone, sweating with fever, physically exhausted from pouring himself out week in and week out (the revival is now into its ninetieth week and Steve preaches all four nights of the weekly meetings, with each service averaging between five and six hours), yet he doesn't let up, he doesn't mention his condition, and he doesn't take a shortcut and find a way to quit early and go home. Why? He is a soldier in his Master's army, there are souls in the balance, and besides, the devil isn't letting up. Why should we? For years I have wondered: If Heaven and hell are real, how can we be real and live the way we do? Steve answers that question emphatically: We are *not* living right and Heaven and hell are hardly real to us, otherwise we *would* live differently. Steve lives differently, but I am convinced that in God's sight, it is quite normal.

I have seen him ready to burst some nights when he sees the building packed with an overflow crowd (lines commonly form at 4:00 a.m. for the 7:00 p.m. services) and wonders, "But how will the sinners get in?" I have seen him chafe when much of the main sanctuary is filled with ministers (he dearly loves Christian workers and is thrilled to have them in attendance) while local punk rockers, prostitutes, drunkards, unsaved homemakers, and lost business people end up in one of the overflow rooms. As a true evangelist, those are the ones he is after and those are the ones he wants to touch. And while all of us rejoice every Friday night when we hear the glorious baptismal testimonies of those transformed in the revival—from lesbians and homosexuals to longtime drug addicts; from church kids gone astray to unconverted ministers—no one rejoices more than Steve. We have often exchanged tearful glances during the revival—sometimes tears of anguish, sometimes tears of fervent prayer and pleading, and sometimes tears of joy. At Brownsville, the tears always flow!

Now it is time for you to enter in. You will not *see* the tears in the eyes of the evangelist as you read, but you will *feel* them. And you will learn one thing very quickly: Steve Hill is after you! You might as well try to escape from the sun at noontime in the desert as try to escape from these messages. They will find you out. They will chase you down. They will demolish your excuses. And they will set you free.

It is always Steve's goal to preach so that an 8-year-old can understand him just as well as an 80-year-old, and you will find these messages to be quite simple—and quite searching. They are clear and to the point as well as convicting and pointed. They are sharp, but if received, soothing. They are merciless toward sin but full of mercy to the sinner. And this evangelist who warns you about hell in no uncertain terms is the same man who answers his phone with the words, "Jesus loves you!" You don't have to live without Jesus and you don't have to die without Jesus. You can live for Him and die with Him, you can know Him, you can serve Him, you can enjoy Him—forever. That's what it's all about, and that's the reason Steve does what he does. He wants to please his Savior, and he wants you to know Him too.

So put your defenses down, open your heart, and get ready to hear the voice of the Lord. Isn't it time for you to have a fresh encounter with the living God?

Dr. Michael L. Brown
February, 1997

Chapter 1

White Cane Religion

It was eight o'clock in the morning when I knocked on the man's door outside of Lansing, Michigan. I just kept knocking until I got an answer. The fellow who finally came to the door was a monster of a man, complete with shaved head, tattoos, and earrings pinned up and down both ears. I looked at this wild maniac of a man and said, "Hi, my name is Steve Hill." He looked at me and said, "My name is Jesse. What do you want?" I peered into his bloodshot eyes and said, "I'm a preacher of the gospel of the Lord Jesus Christ. I want to come in and talk to you."

I'll never forget that morning. I was preaching in the area, and I saw the face of this gang leader plastered across the front page of the morning paper. He looked "as mean as a snake." I asked the pastor of the church hosting the meetings if there was any way we could visit the gang leader pictured on the front page of the newspaper. He said, "As a matter of fact, Steve, I think I know where we can find him."

We drove up to the house early in the morning—I always visit drug addicts and gang members early in the morning because that's when they drag themselves home. By that time, they're tired and beat up, and that's when you want to catch them. Don't try to talk to them when they're about to leave for the night.

When I told this huge man who I was and what I was there for, he shuffled his feet like an awkward teenager. You see, his gang was gone and there weren't any friends around to impress or boost his courage. It was just him and me. He opened the door and sat down without a word, so I followed him in. I figured that since I had already managed to get in there, I might as well go for the gold. I stuck my finger in his face and said, "I know you, Jesse. I know everything about you, man."

He looked at me with a real interesting expression, but I wasn't finished yet. "I want to tell you what your life is like," I said, "You go out at night with a gang of 35 guys and terrorize this county as 'the Viceroy gang.' Your bunch is known as one of the meanest gangs in this whole area. You have vandalized neighborhoods and you have raped girls, and I know it. You have been involved in thievery. You have been involved in grand theft auto. You're involved in fights every night. You go into restaurants and brutalize the people inside."

I looked even more intently into his face and said, "I know all about you, but let me tell you something, Jesse. I also know the man inside you. When you get home and shut the door, you go into that bedroom right over there. When you're all by yourself, you cry yourself to sleep at night. You aren't some great leader; you're just following that bunch of kids around. They pushed you up to the top as a leader, but *everybody is following somebody!*"

Then I sat back and said, "Jesse, you're the unhappiest man on the face of this earth—and you know it. I came here to tell you that."

Do you know what that gang leader did? No, he didn't raise up to hit me, friend. He started bawling like a baby! Do you know what he said? He said, "You know me, man. You know me." How did I know what was going on inside that notorious gang leader? The truth, my friend, is that *everybody is following somebody*. Jesse Martin was just trapped in life. He didn't know where he was going. He needed to surrender his life to Jesus Christ.

The big question is this: "Does the 'somebody' you are following know where he is going?" Jesus gave us a serious warning when He said, "Can the blind lead the blind? shall they not both fall into the ditch?" (Lk. 6:39b) I want to illustrate this message on "white cane religion" the best way I know how. Picture a man with a white cane, wearing sunglasses, tapping his way across a platform in front of people. This is an illustration of a blind person trying to find his way across unfamiliar territory using a white cane.

People who have been deprived of their sight by birth defects, accidents, or disease are totally different from the people caught up in "white cane religion." Individuals who are physically blind would love to receive their sight—they would throw away their canes in a heartbeat if they could see, for they did not become blind by choice. The spiritually blind are a totally different class—the majority are blind by choice.

Many "sighted" people sitting in our church pews each Sunday are totally blind! Most young people are listening to pure garbage, and a lot of Christians are listening to people who have made it their "call in life" to talk against this revival and sway people away from getting more of God. They are going to stand before God and be required to explain their actions on Judgment Day. They will have to explain their blindness and take the blame for being "the blind leading the blind." There are people who literally wanted to get saved at the Brownsville Revival, but before they got out of their front door, some blind guide caught their ear and whispered, "You don't need to go over there. God can touch you right here." (God can touch people anywhere He chooses, but what if He *chooses* to touch them at the Brownsville

Revival—just as He has touched hundreds of thousands already?)

Friend, who are you listening to? Does the one you are listening to know where he's going? Does he even know the Lord? Does he have any idea of what it means to be filled with the Holy Ghost? Who are you listening to?

Every time I preach a message like this, religious people get irritated with me, but I just bless them in the name of the Lord. I'm not irritated with them so why should they be irritated with me? It happens every time I talk about "white cane religion." God gave me this message one morning early in the revival at Brownsville. I usually get to bed around two or three o'clock in the morning on revival meeting nights, and then I get up again at five or six o'clock that morning to get the message for the evening service. People often ask me, "Don't you feel like you're in a pressure cooker most of the time?" When I lay down each night, I say, "Lord Jesus, in just a few hours I'll be getting up. I know You will be ready to speak to my heart and change my life as You give me a message."

I've learned that when I trust Him, there is absolutely no pressure to "perform" or impress people with my theology or preaching ability. I have one goal and one goal only: I want every five-, six-, and seven-year-old child in the audience to understand my message. If the children understand, I know Grandpa will understand what I'm saying too.

I have a little poem the Lord gave me that talks about the lies we tell to justify our blindness:

> You say it's not true. Okay by me. But listen, my friend, and you will see.
>
> There is a pied piper playing loud and clear. It may be fate, but you draw near.
>
> Like a lamb to die, you roam along, unaware of his fateful song.
>
> He lullabies, he hums, he sings, to his destiny your soul he brings.

His cadence heard throughout centuries. Get in line, lift up
your knees.
I'm in charge of this fateful trip. You're in my hands. I've got
a grip,

A grip on you and your best friend. We're going to march until
the end.
Hand in hand we'll walk this road, to the very edge and off
we'll go.

The load will drop and we will too, into a pit, your life is
through.
As you begin to fall headlong, in your heart you'll hear this
childhood song.

Jesus loves me, this I know, for the Bible tells me so.
Little ones to Him belong, they are weak but He is strong.

You'll remember back to early days when life was simple, you
never strayed.
You loved the Lord. You held Him tight, all through the day,
all through the night.

But someone came along in life with a bill of goods, your
soul's the price.
You're so holy, you're so kind, come on, friend, don't be so
blind.

My friends and I are religious too, but we'll have fun before
life's through.
We party, we play, we feed ourselves, on carnal delights, don't
believe in hell.

Material girl, material man—trust me, friend, God understands.
He doesn't expect you to live so clean. Come on, get real, see
what I've seen.

I offered it all to the Lamb of God, fame and fortune everywhere He trod.
But He turned me down, what a fool. Now, here we are, what
about you?

Ah, you've loosened your hold on God's sweet hand, made the
choice, joined this hellish band.
Like all the rest your end is clear. You never suspected your
fate was near.

But it's too late. Go ahead and cry. That's all we hear when
people die.
They come here thinking all was well. "No, not me, I'll never
go to hell."

Into the ditch we watch them fall, as the flames of hell lick up
the walls.
The truth pounds loud in the chambers deep. You had your
chance your soul to keep.

"But I'm not bad as other men, I pay my dues, will till the end.
I tithe, I help sing in the choir. Don't stand there and call me a
liar.

"Of course, I'm not on fire like you. It's your job to preach the
way you do.
I'm just an ordinary child of God. Don't come after me with
your chastening rod."

Please listen up, my friend, tonight, the Spirit of God says,
"Make things right."
He is the One who convicts of sin. The Holy Ghost knows
where you've been.

He knows whether you've been lukewarm. He also knows why
your life is torn.
You've sold out to the other side. You've turned from God to
follow a blind guide.

It's really simple, now is the time, you've listened to this little
rhyme.
Jesus knows, He's been there too. He bled and died to salvage
you.

He snatched the keys of death, the grave. Only in Him your life
  is saved.
So before you leave, walk out these doors, get right with God,
  new life in store.

He'll open your eyes. The blind will see.
Tonight you'll walk in victory.

Everyone on this planet is religious. I don't care if you are
a self-proclaimed agnostic or an atheist; it makes no difference to me. You are religious. The modern definition of "religious" is different from the way our forefathers defined it.
There was a time when "religious" referred to an adherence
to Jesus Christ. If you said a man was religious, you were saying that he was a devoted follower of Jesus.

Today things have changed. Now everyone is religious.
According to *Merriam-Webster's Collegiate Dictionary*, religion
can be "a cause, principle, or system of beliefs held to with
ardor and faith."[1] That means a fisherman is religious. Serious golfers and compulsive Monday night football fans are
religious about their sports. A computer technician is religious about his work. Everyone is religious.

You can say that you don't believe in Jesus Christ, that
you're not a churchgoer, and that you believe "life as we
know it is life as we know it—when it's over, it's over." Your
Bible may be a bass-fishing guide, an ESPN program sched-
ule, or an IBM computer manual, but I'm telling you, friend,
you are religious. A dedicated communist is a religious person. Your religion headquarters can be in the business dis-
trict of downtown New York, and your daily meditations
might be the financial columns in the pages of *The Wall
Street Journal*. You are a religious man. I'm telling you it is
white cane religion. You have latched onto a cause, a belief,
and you are willing to go to bat for what you believe. Yes,
you are religious. But the question is, where is your religion
taking you?

The great preacher Charles Spurgeon warned of two extremes, and he said the truth lies somewhere between them. On one extreme is the rationalist who says that man needs no guide whatsoever. "Is man not noble? Is he not a gifted creature? Can he not reason and judge on his own? He can surely find his own way with no direction from without. Why does man need a teacher? He can learn on his own." These types of people worship self-sufficiency. Their beliefs cause them to be boasters, and they can never condescend to sit at the foot of a master or follow the track of a guide while clinging to their "religion." Consequently, they frequently become erratic, singular, lawless, and unreasonable in their modes of thought and action. I know many people like this. They often wander into the religion of atheism.

Then there are the people who swing to the other extreme: superstition. They say, "I see I need a guide—I will take the one nearest at hand." Why do you think the viewer statistics and income from "psychic hotlines" on TV are sky-rocketing? Right now, even as you read these words, someone is dialing up a 1-900 "psychic" number and blowing his or her hard-earned money on some no-name person in some no-name place who is going to give them some no-purpose prophecy for their lives. Most of those calls go like this: "Hi, my name is Maggie." The so-called spiritual guide on the other end will say something like, "You're a girl," and the astonished person will gasp and say, "Dear God—you're right!" Then the "guide" might get adventurous and say something like, "You ate yesterday." These "psychics" usually say something generic, yet those people on the other end of the line just marvel.

The spiritually blind yield themselves to "instructors" and are often misled because they will follow someone without the slightest consideration of whether or not their leader is a seeing guide or a blind guide. They are weary of thinking for themselves and want someone else to think for them. This is the religion embraced by millions of people who are satisfied with superficial peace. Spurgeon called it "the peace of slumbering stupidity." That describes it perfectly.

Of course, none of this is new. Centuries ago, people faced the same problems in basically the same ways—only the media have changed. Solomon said, "There is no new thing under the sun" (Eccles. 1:9c). Much has been made of the flood of heroin and crack cocaine inundating our nation, but I remember talking to my grandma before she died back in the 1960's. She told me there was a big heroin problem when she was growing up. Grandma said, "Steve, you could buy heroin down at the corner drugstore. Many of my friends were heroin addicts." I thought, *Grandma, are you saying that there was heroin out there when you were a kid?*

The fact is that if it wasn't heroin, then it would be alcohol. If there were no drugs around to misuse and abuse, we would still have problems because there has always been rebellion. In the Old Testament, rebellion was classified as a capital offense—they stoned kids who rebelled against their parents. I often ask the youth, "How many kids here will say, 'Thank God, I don't live back in the Old Testament'?" They usually cheer because they know if we did live under the Old Testament laws, everyone in the room would be dead, and there would be no Brownsville Revival because there would be no people here to experience it!

Everyone needs a guide in life. Lawyers have a saying that goes, "Anyone who represents himself has a fool for a client." Everyone needs a guide. Anyone who attempts to live out his years on earth without the guidance of God is a bigger fool than lucifer.

There is a white-hot fire sweeping across the land of the free and into the homes of the brave, and it is leaving a consuming conviction in the hearts of the hungry. My Christian friend, if you have been swimming around in the mucky waters of mediocrity, now is the time to step out of that polluted pond! You need to walk over to the crystal river of God and dive in. Within seconds, the stench and stain of your decaying religious pollution will be washed away, leaving you clean as a spring shower and free as a bird. If you are willing to obey, then you can be set free right now.

Jesus warned us about a "ditch" that awaits the shuffling lines of the blind tapping their white canes. Spiritually speaking, this ditch is extremely dangerous. It is a bottomless pit, and its slippery walls are continually licked by tormenting flames. This hole called hell reverberates with the terrorized screams and cries of the damned. The continual grating, gnashing, and grinding of teeth is literally a relief from the day-in and day-out torment of the damned in this place God prepared for the devil and his angels. This ditch, this bottomless pit of pain, is never satisfied. Like a carnivorous jungle beast, this vast chasm seems to say, "There is always room for more," and it is constantly awaiting prey to consume.

You say, "How on earth can you preach like this, Steve? Don't you love us?" That is *why* I preach like this. As a loving father, at various times I have had to tell my children, "I don't ever want you to cross the street again without looking both ways. Do you understand me? Your life could depend on it! Now bend over." Why did I correct and warn my children so sternly? Because I love them, and I don't want to lose my children in a tragic accident *that could be prevented by proper correction and warning*! I want my children to be with me all the days of my life. That is why God commands me to warn you of certain damnation. That is why God sends a conviction through the Holy Spirit. I'm warning you to take a good look at your walk with God. Watch out for the ditch!

It breaks my heart to say that even though hundreds of people come forward every night of the revival to receive

Christ and to repent of their sins, there are another two or three hundred people who stiffen their necks and claw their way out of this place to escape God's call. Even as they drag themselves out of the meeting, they are saying, "I have to get outside where there is some fresh air. I need to get away from whatever it is that is all over me."

Friend, it's called the conviction of the Holy Ghost, and you had better thank Him for it. God loves you, and His conviction on your heart is a sign of His love. He is like a doctor who has to "make you feel bad" before you feel good. He often "pokes and prods" you to find out "where it hurts." Once the problem is found, He deals with it. Sometimes He doesn't use any "anesthetic" at all and it hurts. We've had people scream during revival services, and then they often run down to the altar and wail like children who have been disciplined. But the next thing you know, these same people are loving on Jesus and praising God—free as a bird.

Some people really get bothered at this point. If you get bothered by the preaching, then all I can say is, "Good." My job as an ordained minister of God is to make everyone wake up. This evangelist preaches to the lost, but I also stir up the church and everyone who comes into the meeting. One time I told an auditorium full of pastors that I was about to preach on sin, and one hundred heads bowed over on the spot. A sudden conviction hit them, as if the arrows of the Lord had pierced their hearts. These were pastors! They knew the scam was over. God had their number.

Everybody is following somebody—but how many people in the line are totally blind? "You're wrong, Steve. I'm not following anybody." Yes, you are. "No, I'm not." I can tell who you are following by being with you for just a few minutes. Your actions give you away, and your tongue will reveal your system of beliefs the moment you say just a few simple statements. Do you sound like a walking, talking "sitcom"? If you recorded your conversations today, would you sound like a rerun of yesterday's soap operas? Do you ever catch yourself repeating some of the same outrageous statements you heard just a few hours earlier on that 27-inch big screen "prophet" mounted on a pedestal in your living room? Do you snap at people and exhibit violent behavior? Are you basically dishonest with your deepest feelings? I can almost guarantee that you have been hanging around others who are the same way. At the very least, you are feeding on that kind of behavior through your favorite TV programs or music choices. Everybody is following somebody.

"I don't believe that, Steve. I don't even believe in God." If you claim to be an atheist, friend, then you are religious! "But I don't follow God. I'm not a Baptist, a Methodist, or a Catholic—and there's no way I'm a Pentecostal! I just don't believe in all that spirit worship." So you "live your life the best you can, and when it's all over it's all over." Is that you, friend? According to the scholars, you are an "annihilationist." The academics have already categorized you, buddy. Whether you like it or not, *you're part of a religious group.* I know you thought you were a unique individualist out to prove you are nothing more than a highly evolved animal, but you are just another member of a religious group.

You may be a Muslim who confesses "the oneness of God and his prophet Mohammed." You pray five times each day while you face Mecca, and you give alms to the poor and the local mosque. You fast the daylight hours during the month of Ramadan, and you are planning to make your once-in-a-lifetime required pilgrimage to Mecca next year. You are one of the one billion people who pray to Allah each day.

You may pledge your allegiance to "The Nation of Islam," as a Black Muslim under the leadership of the Rev. Louis Farrakhan. It is even more likely that you think everyone should have the freedom to believe the way he or she chooses. You think all beliefs should unite and give themselves to social action.

Millions of Americans—and American Christians—believe that everyone should have the right to choose the way to God that they are most comfortable following. There is only one problem with this popular notion: *Jesus did not give us that right!* If you claim to be a Christian, but you believe and promote this idea, do you realize, that you are anti-Bible? Jesus told His disciples at the Last Supper, "I am the way. I am the truth. I am the life. Regardless of what many would *like* to believe—there is only one way to the Father, and that is through Me. Any questions?" (See John 14:6.)

If you line up with the "one-world church" movement and think everyone should believe the way he or she wants to and that all beliefs should unite and give themselves to social action, then you are chanting the creed of the Unitarians. The problem is that this belief is in direct contradiction to the Bible. You can't have it both ways. A blood-washed Christian cannot be a Unitarian. If you are not blood-washed, then you're going to be swept right into the one-world church in the end.

Who is leading you around, friend? Who is telling you what to do and where to go? Who is telling you how close to get to God or whether you should "get on fire" or not? Who is leading you down the path of life? Jesus said, "Can the blind lead the blind? shall they not both fall into the ditch?" (Lk. 6:39b) Are you willing to put your "guide" or opinions up against the words of Jesus? (That's what you're doing!)

In his book, *From Holy Laughter to Holy Fire: America on the Edge of Revival,* Dr. Michael Brown lists the great church dignitaries, theologians, and leaders who debunked the great revivals of the past. These people ridiculed the revivals that sprang up through the ministries of Charles Finney, Charles Spurgeon, George Whitefield, Charles and John Wesley, along with the Welsh Revival of 1904-1905 and the Asuza

Street Outpouring of 1906. Books were written against all those moves of God, and people published newspaper articles meant to destroy these glorious outpourings. Then, as now, the critics would watch someone get transformed by the power of God and say, "That's not God!" "Don't you dare go there." "Stay away from Wales." "Don't even think about traveling to Cane Ridge, Kentucky." "Stay away from Azusa Street." "Don't bother going to Brownsville." "You better not get involved in that fanatical revival." "God will damn your soul if you go there."

Who is guiding you? When the blind are leading the blind, I call it, "white cane religion." America is wrapped up in it! This nation is as lost as it can be, even though there is a church sitting on almost every street corner. Something is wrong with this picture.

What about your guide? Does your psychic have any clue about eternity? She may be able to tell you what you had for dinner last night, but can she tell you about everlasting damnation tomorrow? Your guru may help you meditate yourself into a sweet moment of temporary mental peace on earth, but can he lead you to everlasting peace in Heaven?

Was it absurd for the Lord to say, "Can the blind lead the blind?" Of course not. Yet that is exactly what's going on in this nation. America is so gullible. Would you ask a blind man to sit behind the steering wheel of your car and then tell him to drive you home? Would you say, "I know you're blind, but would you pilot this plane? I want you to take off, cross the mountain range, and then land on the other side." Would you say, "My friend, I know you are blind, but would you take the helm of my cabin cruiser and take my family for a trip to the Caribbean?" Of course not. Then why have you, and millions of other intelligent Americans, put spiritually blind and bankrupt leaders in front of you to guide your life?

The blind cannot lead the blind, friend. They don't know where they're going. We insist on following the opinions of glamorous movie stars just because they broke all the box-office records. We hang on every word of champion cowboys, great "space fighters" from our favorite TV series, or the recording artists with the best-selling albums and the most outrageous lifestyles of sin. Suddenly the famous celebrity is an authority on everything.

When a talk show host asks the 26-year-old "star" with a pretty face and a bankrupt personal life, "What do you believe about religion?" she says to the adoring masses, "[Tap, tap, tap...] I believe that God loves everyone. I believe that if all the young people would begin to take a good look at the hatred in their hearts and rid themselves of any bitterness or bias that may have been placed there through their childhood, I believe that they will become united. And together we can become a strong nation once again. And God (whoever he or she may be) will be pleased with us." Then millions of mesmerized viewers bow down and say, "Yes! If I could only be like him or her!"

Meanwhile, pastors across the nation warn their flocks, "[Tap, tap, tap...] Listen to me, congregation. I am an authority, for the degrees on my wall tell me so. You do not have to get so fanatical about your Christian walk that you're out on the streets and in the marketplace testifying, witnessing, and talking about God every hour of the day. God can handle that Himself. He's got angels to do that work. And by the way, why are you so vocal in your worship? Don't be such emotional creatures when it comes to expressing your love to God. I know. After all, I'm your pastor [tap, tap, tap...]."

Does the person you are following know where he's going? If you are following a person, you may be in danger of damning your soul to hell. Are you debating whether or not to get saved or to get on fire for God today because you are afraid your spouse, your parents, or your friends might disapprove?

What about God's opinion? Who cares what people think! On the final day, you will stand alone before God Almighty and be asked to explain why you rejected God's Son and disobeyed His direct command. (No excuse will be good enough then!)

We listen to man-made heroes, leaders, and geniuses like they are spiritual authorities, but only God opens blinded eyes. You may even be a born-again believer in Christ who is wrapped up in the misguided anti-Bible opinions of so-called "authorities on revival." They are busy publishing books and magazine articles and spouting off on television and radio about how "dangerous" revival is to your soul. They work day and night blasting everything God is doing across the world because it doesn't fit into their idea of what is "in order and proper." I grieve for these church leaders. They are leading a couple million critical people who rejoice, saying, "Thank you! Now I have a book—a 'bible of *true* revival' that can go along with my King James and my New American Standard. Now, I can read about your coming revival." (It's obvious it is never coming.)

Who are you listening to? Pastor, if you are a critical man, and if you like to surround yourself with other critical people, then you are steadily tap, tap, tapping your way into a deadly ditch. Why? Every time you meet with your equally critical friends for an hour, you just rip your brethren to shreds—and that's called spiritual mayhem. Mayhem refers to destruction and mutilation. You are literally mutilating the Body of Christ, and there's a price to pay for that sin against God. Each time you meet to shred God's servants, you are all just tapping your blind man's canes in a row as you inch closer and closer to the ditch.

The best thing you can do is to invite someone into that circle who is on fire! Get somebody in that circle who will irritate all of you and go against the grain of doubt and unbelief!

Revival is sweeping this nation because people are sick and tired of the criticism. I counsel you to jump off that religious boat quickly because it is sinking. People who come up to me to criticize are just polluting the air. I've been around the clean air of Heaven, and I don't want that other foul smell around me. There are millions of people out there like me—we want a fresh breath from the presence of God.

Some of the things God says make us so uncomfortable that we make up our own words to avoid the pain. Millions of people are told, "You're okay. You're just going through a hard time," when they should be told, "The truth is that you are in *sin*. You are a *sinner*, and once you realize it and repent, then it will become healing to your bones." We have to admit something is wrong and get a diagnosis before we can get the prescription to make us whole. Unfortunately, too many people are getting a vague analysis that pats them on the back and perpetuates their sin. "Well, my son has been passing through this armed robbery phase for eight years. He'll come out of it. It will pass."

For decades, America has bought the line, "Love your kids—don't spank them. Intelligent, civilized people don't spank their children (only religious fanatics do that). You will harm your children if you spank them!" Now we're dealing with the uncontrollable "Dr. Spock generation of the unspanked hellions."

America got drowsy and has let someone—*anyone*—else do the driving. Who have you put in the driver's seat of your car? Bob Ayala is a friend of mine. He is a profound songwriter and recording artist who loves the Lord with all his heart. He also happens to be physically blind. Hearing this message, he would say, "Preach it, Steve! You would never put me behind the wheel to drive your car." Unspanked hellions and lost adults in rebellion are the fruits of "white cane religion." I want no part of it.

The Gospel of John, chapter 3, describes a white cane tapper who got his spiritual eyes opened to the truth. Nicodemus was a respected member of the Jewish Sanhedrin, one of the "old blind dogs" of religious circles. God was about to teach the "old dog" some new tricks. Nicodemus had probably spent most of the day talking to other respected "blind guides" who were, no doubt, shredding this Jesus of Nazareth. However, he decided to find out himself about Jesus. So he got up, put on his shades, pulled out his long white cane, and went on his search. Tap, tap, tap… "Has anybody seen Jesus of Nazareth?"

Jesus identified Himself, and I can see old Nicodemus saying, "Jesus, is that You? You know me, don't You? I'm Nicodemus. I've been talking with the other leaders, and…I believe You are sent from God. After all, nobody can do the things You do unless they are sent from God. Would You help me? Can You tell me who I am? Why am I here and where am I going?" Nicodemus was basically telling Jesus in John 3:2-21, "I know all this religion stuff is garbage. We don't know what we're talking about. No one does the signs and wonders like You do, Lamb of God. Who am I? Why am I here?" Jesus told this great ruler of Israel, "Ye must be born again" (Jn. 3:7b). I love that story because it shows what can happen to a blind man who comes to Jesus with an honest question and an open heart. God touched Nicodemus that evening, and He wants to touch you and me today.

I believe God wants to see the front platforms and altars of all His churches littered with discarded white canes! The scales are going to fall from blind eyes all across this country and people are going to walk out of bondage and into the light of day—all they have to do is believe God's Word. When they do, their old blind buddies aren't going to believe what has happened to them. They will hear their old blind guides say, "Now wait just a minute. What in the world are you talking about? *I'm the guide around here!*" And Nicodemuses around the country will reply, "Oh no, you don't understand. I can see! I don't need a white cane anymore. I've been born again!"

God is saving a lot of smart people in this revival, and it is bothering a lot of parents and family members who don't know God. Teenagers are going home and telling Mom and Dad, "I went to Brownsville... When the preacher started talking about sin, my heart started pounding and I didn't know what it was. The preacher told us that funny feeling in our hearts would go away if we would just come down to the altar and ask Jesus to wash our sins away. I went down to that altar and in just 30 seconds, something came over me. Mama, I'll never be the same! I'm happy! I'm free!"

Some of them will hear their parents say, "We don't go for all that stuff. That was a Pentecostal church, wasn't it, boy? They don't know any more about God than the man in the moon. We'll teach you. You're 21 years old and you can make it in life, so don't get religion. We can guide you. Follow us, son." (Tap, tap, tap....)

"Sorry, Mama. I've got Jesus in my heart now. My eyes are open. I don't want any 'white cane religion' now." Jesus wants to open your eyes, friend. This isn't about some empty religion that just hangs around the cross. This is true Christianity that climbs onto the cross.

When I got saved, hundreds of my blind friends went tapping down the highway while I made a decision to drop my cane and went dancing the other way. My friends said things like, "You're a fool." I just wanted to tell them, "You idiots, don't you want to see too?" That's why we plead with people at the grocery stores, at the marketplace, and in every service to come to Jesus so their eyes will be opened.

You may be wrapped up in your problems or in the life you're living right now, but God wants to open up your eyes. Your problem is not your work, your relationships with people, the economy, or your empty bank account. Your problem isn't your lack of education or a supposedly low intelligence quotient. Your problem is that you are not close to Jesus. If you'll seek first the Kingdom of God and His righteousness, all these things will be added unto you (see Mt. 6:33).

Some of the greatest preachers in the world could barely speak their native language, yet they managed to shake tens of thousands of people when they proclaimed Christ. D.L. Moody was one of them. He shook the multitudes, and he said it was because he was just a common man with an uncommon God. When D.L. Moody spoke, people listened, because they knew he had his eyes opened. He was different than the blind scribes and Pharisees who were pushing empty religion.

It's time for us to turn in our white canes and drop our dark eyeglasses at the altar. If you know you are blind, then this is the day your eyes will be opened. Jesus Christ has the power to open your eyes, but you have to drop all the trappings of a blind man. Jesus Christ doesn't want part of your life; He wants to *become* your life. He wants it all. He wants to heal your blindness, open your eyes, and change everything for you.

If you are tired of blindness and of being led astray, then ask Jesus Christ to heal your spiritual eyes. Ask Him to be the Lord and Master of your life, to be your Guide. If you are afraid of tomorrow, then take His hand. Jesus is already there in your tomorrow. He knows everything that is going to happen, and He will be your Guide. If you have wandered away from God, then you need forgiveness. If you have never known the Lord, then you need to meet the One who opens up blinded eyes, friend. Meet the One who has set multiplied thousands of blind men and women free in this revival alone over the last few months. We've collected untold thousands of white canes at the altar.

Religion will damn you to hell because it cannot save you. Don't tell me how much you *know about* the Lord. Tell me if you *know* the Lord. Do you wake up in the morning with Jesus on your heart? Do you go to sleep at night with Jesus on your heart? Do you sing His praises through the day? Is He your love? Is He everything to you? Do you worship Him? Do you know Him?

"Well, Steve, our church believes if you're baptized as an infant and confirmed when you're 12 years old, then you're going to go..." Are you going to stand before God one day and say, "God, You know what denomination I'm from, and You know what we believe..." God's Word in Matthew 7:23 says that the Lord will say, "Depart from Me. I never knew you." Case closed. Next.

If something has severed you from God, be careful: It can damn you forever! It might be pornography, witchcraft, or the love of money. It could be a drug habit, rebellion, or some other favorite sin you just don't want to give up. You need to come back to God right now. If you are away from the Lord, then this is your opportunity to come to Jesus. Perhaps your eyes are glazed over. You're not totally blind. You can still see a little bit, but the further you get away from God, the darker it gets. Somehow this book ended up in your hands. You are seeing for the first time in a long time and the scales are beginning to come off. I'm warning you that if you don't act now and repent, then those scales will crust over and totally blind your eyes. God wants to set you free, but you have to do your part.

Jesus loves you and has a plan for your life. He has your attention right now—and He wants you to drop the white cane of religion this very moment. Everybody believes in something. Everybody follows somebody, friend. But who are you following? Who are you listening to? You know without a shadow of a doubt that you need to follow Jesus Christ. You know that everything else is hogwash. Mystics are coming to Jesus to get saved, right alongside witches, intellectuals, and powerful government officials. When the Lord gripped them, they realized that all their intelligence wasn't enough to heal their blindness; they needed the Lord.

Come to the cross and ask the Lord Jesus to open up your blinded eyes, forgive you of your sins, and wash them all away. You're out there groping around, and the whole time someone is trying to help you see. God is dealing with your heart. Don't hesitate. Listen to your heart, friend. See, there's a warfare going on right now and I'm a man of war. I'm a violent man and I'm not going to give up on you. Don't let any distraction keep you from obeying God.

Too many times people act like they are in the food court of a shopping mall where everybody has their hands full and is in a hurry. They think they have automatic permission to lie to one another! When someone asks how they're doing, they say, "Fine. And you?" They don't mention that their family is falling apart, their spouse is leaving them, and the kids are on drugs. No sir, everything is not "fine." Don't lie. Friend, if you need to ask Jesus Christ to wash those sins away, if you know you're separated from the Lord right now, then tell the truth to the Holy Spirit and say out loud, "Yes, I need forgiveness."

On certain nights at the revival, I see hundreds of people come to be saved as soon as I call them down. On other nights, the "tapping" sound is almost deafening. Some people have a death grip on their white cane religion and the devil is sitting on their laps. There may be a hellish bondage on you as you struggle to read these words. I have to warn you that if you go to hell, it will only be because you wanted it with all your heart, soul, and strength. If that's what you really want, then that is exactly what you will get. If you lay down this book and walk away blind, it will be because you chose to. Don't wait any longer, friend. You need to learn about the patience of God. It has its limits! I must tell you that a loving Savior will one day be a severe Judge.

Drop the white cane and the dark glasses that hide your blindness. Bare you blind eyes so the Healer can touch them and restore your spiritual sight. Today is the day of salvation—not tomorrow, not next week, not next year. Obey today. If you are ready to receive your sight and follow the Giver of Life, then pray this prayer out loud right now, right where you are. God is listening:

Dear Jesus, thank You for speaking to my heart. Thank You for not leaving me alone. I need You. Open my eyes so I can see; I don't want to be blind anymore. I want to see clearly.

Lord Jesus, I have sinned and I have broken Your heart. I've wronged You and I've hurt others. Forgive me and wash my sins away. I ask You to be my Lord, my Savior, and my very best friend.

From this moment on I will follow You. You are my Guide. I'm throwing away my white cane religion. Instead, I will follow You all the days of my life. I pray this in Your precious name. Amen.

If you have prayed this prayer and meant it from your heart, then you have something important to share with your friends. I know of one young high school graduate who spent all her graduation money just to get her friends to the revival in Pensacola. She wanted to give her best friends the same wonderful gift she had received from Jesus—eternal life. I've heard hundreds of stories like that, and more are taking place every week. Friend, when God changes your life, you just have to share it!

End Note

1. *Merriam Webster's Collegiate Dictionary*, 10th ed. (Springfield, MA: Merriam-Webster, Inc., 1994) 988.

Chapter 2

Counterfeit Conversion

I'll never forget the night I went to a "Jesus people" Bible study in 1971. I was a junior in high school, and just as wild as I could be. I'd been busted several times, and I lived just like many of my friends who died over the next few years. I was a drug addict and into the partying scene.

A friend from California was running the Bible study, and he was a natural leader. I was a non-believer, but I really respected this guy, so I went to his Bible study with about 50 other people. I sat there listening to the preaching and teaching, and I watched everybody else pray. I liked what was happening, so when the Bible study was over I waited around. *I probably would have been saved that night if it hadn't been for what I saw in the next few minutes....*

I saw my friend slip out with his girlfriend, so I followed them over to his house and went in. When I walked back to the bathroom, I saw this Bible study leader whom I respected so much pumping heroin into a distended vein in his arm. It was blatant hypocrisy in its worst form. I walked out of that place thinking, *If this is Christianity, I don't want any part of it!*

I know my experience was an extreme case, but it really affected me. In fact, it probably caused many of my friends who died over the next two years to be ushered into hell. If

I had met Jesus that night, I know I would have been instrumental in bringing my friends to that Bible study and to the Lord. Instead, my friend's hypocrisy totally turned me off to the gospel and to Jesus Christ. I believe that sin and hypocrisy caused the Jesus Movement as a whole to dissipate sooner than it should have because God will not put up with that kind of junk. His truth will reign—period. God will never bless sin.

For many years, my wife Jeri and I took drug addicts and troubled young people into our home to live with us. Why? We sure didn't do it for entertainment! No, we wanted peace and quiet just like everybody else, but we cared about people and we wanted them to see genuine, real-life Christianity. When Jesus saved us, He put His love in us. It is love that drives us to work and minister night after night until two or three in the morning in this revival. This is grueling work, and people often ask, "How do you do it?" It's by the grace and the power of the Lord.

It can be difficult when your preaching begins to pry into people's lives, but the greatest growth in my life came from preaching like that. Leonard Ravenhill was one of my favorite preachers. During the years I sat under his ministry, he was always "prying" into my life. He would always nail me by sticking his finger in my face and saying, "Stevie, how much have you been praying?" He nailed me right there because I knew better than to lie.

David Wilkerson was the same way. He would always nail us for things that were going on in our lives. I can still hear him tell us, "If you're not closer to Jesus today than you were yesterday, you've backslid." I used to hate hearing that, but I needed it. Now I'm telling more than ten thousand people a week at the revival, "Examine yourself." We have a generation of young people out there who don't even believe in hell or judgment. They don't believe in the wrath of God. Kids on the streets will tell you that when they die, God is going to look at them and "understand." Or worse, they will look at you and flippantly say, "I'm going to hell, and so are all my friends." When people make foolish statements like that, they don't believe in hell (and they definitely don't know anything about it).

This nation is sick of counterfeit conversions and counterfeit Christianity. The world says, "We're sick of the hypocrites in the church." Sure these worldly people are hypocrites too, and they have probably done their share of sinning. But the bottom line is that there *is* a lot of hypocrisy in the "church." There are people who say they know the Lord but don't. Virtually everybody in this nation "believes" in Jesus. ("Yeah, He existed.") That's not the point. Do you *know* Him? The Jesus of the Bible nailed people to the wall, and He irritated folks, friend. Yes, He's wonderful, but He also chased people out of the temple with a whip. Listen to His words:

> *Woe unto you, scribes and Pharisees, hypocrites! for ye make clean the outside of the cup and of the platter, but within they are full of extortion and excess. Thou blind Pharisee, cleanse first that which is within the cup and platter, that the outside of them may be clean also. Woe unto you, scribes and Pharisees, hypocrites! for ye are like unto whited sepulchres, which indeed appear beautiful outward, but are within full of dead men's bones, and of all uncleanness. Even so ye also outwardly appear righteous unto men, but within ye are full of hypocrisy and iniquity* (Matthew 23:25-28).

Those are some hard words from the Prince of Peace. The apostle Paul warned Timothy:

> *This know also, that in the last days perilous times shall come. For men shall be lovers of their own selves, covetous, boasters, proud, blasphemers, disobedient to parents, unthankful, unholy, without natural affection, trucebreakers, false accusers, incontinent, fierce, despisers of those that are good, traitors, heady, highminded, lovers of pleasures more*

than lovers of God; having a form of godliness, but denying the power thereof: from such turn away (2 Timothy 3:1-5).

"Having a form of godliness...." Now, a counterfeit is made as an imitation of something else with the intent to deceive. It is an inferior imitation or copy. It is a sham, something that is likely to be confused with the genuine article. My son bought a black cellular telephone for two dollars that looks absolutely genuine. What if that counterfeit cellular telephone was sitting on the counter in someone's home while a babysitter was watching the kids—and a fire broke out in the house or an accident occurred? The panicked babysitter might see that cellular phone on the counter and think, *This is a lifesaver!* It looks like a phone. It feels like a phone. It even lights up, dials, and beeps like a real cellular phone. As smoke fills the house, or while she frantically tries to stop the bleeding of a wound, this woman might dial 911 and hear the reassuring beeps as the phone in her hand apparently begins to make the life-saving contact with emergency personnel. There is only one problem—the phone is a fake!

All over America, people are dying and going to hell because they've entrusted their lives to counterfeit converts, fake messiahs, and false "truths." There are going to be killings today because of counterfeits! Somewhere today in our nation, some kid is going to point a black plastic play gun at a cop and go, "Bang, bang." The cop will react the way he is trained to act when he sees a "deadly weapon" pointed toward him. He reacts with deadly force and shoots back at the kid. When the shocked cop walks over to examine his attacker, he will find he has shot a child armed with a weapon bearing the "Made by Mattel" stamp at the bottom. This has really happened!

There are factories around the world that make fake products. Plants in Russia crank out fake "Levi jeans" by the thousands, and if you buy a "Sharp" brand watch on the black market, it looks like a Sharp. It ticks like a Sharp. It plays music like a Sharp. But if you get real close and look at the brand name, it doesn't say "Sharp." It says "Shapp." It's not the genuine article, friend. It will break down on you. Unfortunately, there are also churches and ministries around the world that crank out counterfeit conversions.

During the years I spent in Argentina, we often had short-term missionary groups came down from the States to help build church buildings. These visitors were always tempted to buy the Rolex watches on sale down there for $35. Yes, they look just like genuine $8,000 Rolex watches, but they are not the real thing. I remember one man who bought one. His watch ticked like a Rolex, and it looked like a Rolex. But when we were on our way to the airport, this brother looked down at his new watch and saw one of the hands fall off! He said, "Brother Steve, look at this watch, man." When he showed it to me, I watched the other hand fall off! He said, "I don't think this is a real Rolex." I told him, "You're right, buddy."

My favorite U.S. city is New York. You can stand on any New York City street corner and just be entertained all day. I love to watch the folks who open up coats that are just lined from top to bottom with "genuine" gold watches and jewelry. They may have a "genuine Seiko, 17-jewel, calendar watch" with a glistening gold band for only $9.95! If a potential customer says, "You've got to be kidding," they'll quickly answer, "No sir, I'm running a special today." If the seller senses a potential sale, he'll usually ask, "Where are you from?" Whether your answer is Texas, Vietnam, or Fifth Avenue, he'll say something like, "Texas? We're running a dollar off for everyone from Texas today!"

Christianity is the same way. We have fallen for cheap imitations of what is real. We have substituted low-cost fakes for the high-cost truth. Too many of us have fallen for religion because it satisfied the little craving we had inside. However, once you experience and taste the real thing in a genuine revival meeting, you will feel almost like you have been ripped off.

While we were planting a church in Granada, Spain, I decided to take a convert from Ireland with me to do some snorkeling along the beautiful Mediterranean coast of Spain. The road I took was picturesque, and every city along the way had a castle. We turned a corner and saw a beautiful ravine leading down to a perfect snorkeling spot in the emerald waters of a small protected inlet. It was hard work climbing down to the water's edge, but we were headed for what looked like one of the best snorkeling spots in the Mediterranean!

I am sure that very few people had ever visited that inlet on foot. My friend, Mark, put on his diving mask and fins first, so I said, "You go first." He was in the water no more than 30 seconds before he came out screaming! That poor guy had discovered there were dead fish floating all over the place just under the surface. A rag had wrapped itself around one of his feet, and he said the place was filled with pollution and trash! I could not believe it at first, but when we took a closer look, we realized the whole place was polluted. Yet from the surface, it had looked like a snorkeler's paradise.

Things can look a whole lot different when you get a little bit closer. That is what God is doing with His Church today. He's getting a little bit closer. No, He doesn't need to move closer so He can see—He is moving closer so *we* can see our sorry reflection compared to His perfect countenance. We need to see underneath the surface. We want to move on to the deeper things of God, but first we must let the Lord's cleansing fire burn all the way through.

The reason so many people are staying in this revival is because we're getting fruit that remains. I remember hearing a true story about some Romanian Christians who had gathered for a church service during the days of violent Communist oppression in their country. The service was going along normally when, suddenly, two heavily armed Communist soldiers burst into the church and locked the doors behind them. Everyone froze. Then the soldiers announced, "We are going to kill you! If you remain faithful to Jesus, we will shoot you here and now. But if you want to deny Him, we will let you leave."

You could have heard a pin drop in that startled room. At first, no one moved, but after a little while, a few of the believers got up and left as the soldiers opened the doors for them. The rest stayed. They were ready to die for their faith.

Then the soldiers locked the doors again and turned to the faithful believers still sitting in their pews. This was it! But instead of pointing their rifles at the heads of the Christians, they put the rifles down! Then they said, "Praise God! We are Christians too. But we could not risk worshiping God with anyone who was not willing to die for his faith." Then they had church together!

Can you imagine how the folks felt who got up and left, only to hear later that it was all a hoax? It was a good litmus test of faith and dedication to Christ. Those who left cared more for this present life than they did for Jesus. How would you do in this kind of test?

How do you know if you're a counterfeit convert? Number one, *if you serve God for what you can get out of Him*, you are a counterfeit convert. You are playing poker with Heaven because you want to win something for nothing. You are constantly asking yourself, "What can I get out of God? What does He have for me?"

The truth is that apart from God, you and I are not worth a nickel. The Bible says your righteousness has the same value and quality as filthy rags, so you really don't have a thing to "bargain with" (see Is. 64:6). Counterfeit converts come to God with excuses and lies. Genuine converts come to the Lord on their knees, fall on their faces before Almighty God, and pray, "God, if You can see fit to even glance my way, have mercy on me, a sinner."

Counterfeit converts don't obey God because they love Him, but because they hope to get something out of Him for their own gain. Counterfeit converts often show up at revivals. Since we have a lot of pretty girls coming to the revival at Brownsville Assembly of God, we also see a lot of boys show up for services. I've seen a lot of men come to church and get "saved" just to impress or win a woman's heart. They even get involved in Bible study, give real money during the offerings, and show up at every church service—until they finally marry the woman they've been pursuing. Once the chase is over, things usually take a sudden "U-turn." The next thing you know, our "wonder convert" suddenly disappears from the church scene, and the woman he married backslides! The woman usually can't believe what has happened to her. It was all a counterfeit conversion, friend. The "wonder convert" was really a counterfeit who only served God for what he could get out of Him.

Listen, Jesus has done enough for you and me. He doesn't have to do a thing more. To borrow a phrase from the late John F. Kennedy, "Ask not what Jesus can do for you, but ask what you can do for Jesus!"

The second mark of a counterfeit convert is that *he only does what he has to do, even though it's not what he really wants to do.* "I *have* to go to church. I can't smoke anymore (but I want to). I can't drink anymore (but I'd like to)." Why? He'll say, "Because I'm a Christian now." Baloney! You have never been a genuine Christian, friend. It is all counterfeit if you serve God because you *have* to, not because you really want to. A genuine convert may be tempted, and for a moment his flesh may want to sin, but deep down, he will really want to please

God. This is why he will quickly turn away from the wrong path—unlike the counterfeit convert, the genuine convert really wants to please God.

People often ask me how I quit hard drugs. "Was it hard, Brother Steve? After all, you were a junkie, man. You were a mainliner! Was it hard to kick dope and quit smoking three packs of cigarettes a day?" Friend, when you fall in love with Jesus, things change. When I got saved, God delivered me from my drug habit. But no one "made me" cut my hair or quit drinking. No one made me quit smoking, either. As a matter of fact, the Christians I got around never mentioned that stuff or blasted me with condemnation. All they said was, "God loves you and He has a plan for your life. Your body is the temple of the Holy Ghost, Steve, so take care of it." I thought, *Wow, my body is the temple of the Holy Ghost!* I wanted to take care of my body from that moment on. True Christianity is rooted in a "want to" motivation. You *want* to serve God because He first loved you!

The world is sick and tired of "have to" religion, and Jesus was nauseated with it too! I believe the Lord's stomach churned when He saw religious hypocrisy. He basically told some high-ranking religious hypocrites in Matthew 23, "You're whitewashed tombs full of dead men's bones. You don't love God. You do all this because you have to, so people will look at your piety and say how wonderful you are." Do you want to know why first-century Jewish burial sepulchers were whitewashed? They held the remains of important people. These burial places were whitewashed so people who walked by would see the whitewashed grave and associate it with holiness. They wanted people to think, "Oh, that's where that pious priest is buried. That's where ole Jim is. God rest his soul. He was so holy." Jesus was blunt. He said, "They're full of dead men's bones. They didn't live for God; they never knew Him, and they never will." He was sick of it, and the world is too.

I believe that a great awakening and revival is about to sweep through this country, but it has to come from pure Christianity—from real people who live for God, who walk and talk and live in His presence day in and day out. We need to live the same way at home as we do at church. My wife Jeri and I have had people live with us for long periods of time. Let me assure you that the "real you" comes out quickly at home. One young lady who lived with us for almost a year is now a missionary in Africa. Jeri led her to the Lord. She saw Christianity lived out in our home every day, and she heard everything we said. If I said in a meeting that I get up at five every morning to seek God, she *knew* whether or not it was true! It's easy to say a thing in public, but do you follow through in private—even when no one but God is watching?

Jesus has been living in your home from the beginning. He knows what goes on in secret, so it is time to be real. If you are like so many others who "came to the Lord with a group," but never personally committed to Him, then you need to make sure you have made Jesus Christ your Lord and Savior. If you secretly wonder whether or not you are saved, stop worrying this moment. End the questions by repenting of your sins and asking the Lord Jesus to forgive you and save your soul. He will wash you clean and make you brand-new.

If this revival at Brownsville is known for one thing around the world, it is known for *true conversions* that are backed up by the proof of *changed lives*. The "Brownsville Revival" has produced thousands of conversions and is recognized for the deep levels of repentance, brokenness, and awe-filled worship it produces in the lives of those touched by God in its services. The conversions are real, and they bring forth real, lasting fruit.

The third mark of a counterfeit convert is that his basic motivation is fear, not love. He is not only afraid of hell, but he also fears punishment, judgment, and disgrace in man's eyes as well. Don't be deceived. The counterfeit convert is not living for God. He is still living for himself. He thinks of himself first and seeks his own happiness and safety before any other consideration. His fear of hell and punishment keeps him outwardly moral, but his brand of self-made obedience is formal, heartless, loveless, and completely worthless.

Many convicted felons who are released from prison on probation forget all about the rules they agreed to follow in return for a taste of freedom—until it all starts to catch up with them. When the probation officer threatens to send the prisoner back to prison, all of a sudden the parolee shows up at local shopping malls, in church, and on the street dressed up in a nice suit. They are "toeing the line" because they know they're about to get busted. The law is about to come down on them, and all of a sudden they remember the judge's warning, "If you violate parole again by hanging around your old dope-dealing friends, if you get caught carrying a gun again, or if you fail to show up for your weekly appointment with the parole officer, you're going right back to your cell." A lot of Christians act the same way. When we feel like we're about to get caught (as if we can fool God for even one second!), then we try to "straighten up for awhile." That is so counterfeit. We need to get real, friend. God is looking at our *hearts*.

A lot of us are like my son's counterfeit cellular telephone, or those $35 imitations of the $8,000 Rolex watches—we look like the real thing, but we aren't. We're fakes, we're counterfeits, having an outward "form of godliness" without the power of God. Counterfeit Christians don't know the Lord; they only know *about* Him.

True revival creates and thrives on honest relationships with God and man. We've had badge-wearing, Bible-toting pastors come to the altar to give their hearts to the Lord *for the first time* in this revival. God demands honesty in ministry. Once these precious men submitted their lives to Jesus

Christ in truth, they were ready to genuinely lead their flocks toward God.

I was preaching at one of the most respected inner-city churches in America recently when the pastor stood before his own congregation on a Sunday morning and confessed, "I just want to share with this church that I tried to get a message for this Sunday morning service. But the heavens were brass all day yesterday because in the morning I screamed at my wife. I yelled at her so harshly that she ran to our bedroom, fell on the bed, and cried before God—all because of my cruelty." Then this spiritual leader said, "I went to my study, shut the door, and actually prayed, 'God, speak to me about the service tomorrow.' No way. The heavens were brass."

Then this pastor whom I deeply respect stepped away from the pulpit and publicly fell on his knees in front of his wife and said, "Forgive me, darling. I love you so much. Forgive every word that came out of my mouth, honey." When this man confessed his fault in front of his congregation and publicly asked for forgiveness, the place just erupted. Why? Because it was *real*!

People are sick of counterfeit Christianity. They're sick of all this false piety parading around as the real thing. They want to see your honesty. They want to see the real thing. This country is waiting for true Christianity.

Before I was a Christian, I knew I was a heathen. But then someone told me about Jesus. He changed my whole life. Perhaps you haven't had a chance to be a counterfeit Christian because you have never known God. You've been real; you've just been a heathen. You are in sin, but you're not faking it. Now is your chance to meet and experience the Real Thing—Jesus.

This country is sick of the hypocrisy. Jesus is sick of it. And it's about time you get sick of it. Night after night I watch people come forward to meet Jesus, carrying bags of demonic groceries. They are burdened down with sin, disappointment, and bitterness. But when they meet Jesus, they leave those bags of pain behind and dance out of the place because they are so free.

I believe people need to come to Jesus Christ the same way He died for them on the cross—publicly, boldly, and in front of everybody. It has to be real. Anything less is going to be counterfeit. We only create "closet Christians" when we tell people they can accept Jesus by "raising their right index finger" so no one else can see their commitment. I demand the real thing because Jesus deserves the real thing.

Some of us have been serving God like we take medicine— we only take enough to get what we want out of Him. If this is you, then you need to repent and say, "Jesus, I'm so sick of this. All I do is wheel and deal with You, and I spend most of my time complaining because You don't answer my prayers the way I think You should. I'm going to fall on my face this time. Do whatever You want to do with me all the days of my life—I'm content from this moment on. No more counterfeit, Jesus."

Even when Paul the apostle was bobbing like a cork out in the open sea during a storm, he was just as content as he was when he was preaching to multitudes on dry ground. It didn't matter to him. He said, "I have learned, in whatsoever state I am, therewith to be content" (Phil. 4:11b). He might have put it this way today: "Whether there's a T-bone steak on my plate or a piece of stale bread, I'm happy, Jesus." Like Paul, you should serve God because you love Him. Examine yourself. Are you really in the faith? Paul said, "Work out your own salvation with fear and trembling" (Phil. 2:12b).

There is a whole lot more to the Christian life than one "abracadabra prayer" mumbled under your breath one Sunday morning in 1980 or 1997! No, the real thing—genuine

Christianity—involves a serious walk with the Lord. If God is speaking to you, if you feel like He has touched your heart, then you need to *do something* about it. Ask the Lord to forgive you, wash you clean, and give you a fresh start right now.

Be honest. No counterfeit conversions or fakes allowed. If you're a prodigal, if you want to come back home to Jesus, if you're a counterfeit convert who is tired of the false life, then pray right now. But don't play games. False piety can fool a thousand people, but it won't fool God. If you want God to touch you, if you are hungry for the real thing, then tell the Lord, "Jesus, I am sick and tired of this. I want to change."

You will go after what you want. If you are really hungry and thirsty for God, then you will pursue God. You say, "But I'm already a Christian." Let me ask you one question: Has someone ever walked up to you with a tract and told you that Jesus loves you and has a plan for your life? What was your reaction? Were you offended that someone would witness to you as if people somehow are supposed to know by your smell and clothing that you are a Christian? Did you quickly tell him, "I'm saved. I go to the Methodist church. I do this. I do that"? You should have told him, "You blessed my soul. I need to be doing what you're doing out at this mall, rather than showing all this false piety."

Examine yourself right now, friend. Look inside your heart. Does your life have the marks of a counterfeit Christian life, or is it the real thing? If it is the real thing, then you'll live for the Lord because you love Him, not because you have to. Not because you are afraid. Not just for the benefits you get from God. Pray this prayer right now:

Lord Jesus, I want my Christian experience to be real from this moment on. I want it to be real. I'm sick and tired of living in fear, of being afraid of being punished by God. I want to live right because I want to please You.

If you do something wrong, don't fake it or put up a false front to hide your sin. Just fall on your face and say, "Jesus, I am so sorry. Please forgive me." He will forgive you because He promised He would. Don't pray this prayer out of fear; pray it because you love Him.

It is no accident that you are reading these words at this moment. Either you want to get your heart right with God, or you want to get closer to Jesus, or you will be ministering to people who need and want to do these things. Your heart has been stirred by this message. Perhaps you have been backslidden for a long time—God wants you to come back home. If you left the Father's house, lived a terrible life, and landed in a dead end going nowhere, then listen: You've made it back home. It is time to look up. Your heavenly Father is waiting for you right now. His arms are wide open to welcome you home.

Maybe you've been there every time your church doors opened, but now you're afraid you've been a fake all along. God knows what you really are and what you've really done, but He also knows what is in your heart right now. If you really want to change, I want you to pray this prayer out loud right now:

Dear Jesus, thank You for speaking to my heart. I don't want to be a counterfeit; I want to be real. Thank You for coming to this earth as the genuine Son of God. I'm glad You lived a perfect life and that You were never a counterfeit.

You went to the cross and died the terrible death that I deserved—You took my punishment in my place. Your death and resurrection were not counterfeit; they were the real thing. Thank You. I want the same thing in my life. I ask You to forgive me and wash my sins away. I repent of every wrong thing I have done. Please forgive me, Lord.

I ask You to be my Lord, my Savior, and my very best friend. From this moment on, I am Yours one hundred percent, and You are mine one hundred percent. I will serve You out of love, not fear. I thank You for loving me, Jesus. In Your precious name. Amen.

Chapter 3

Stubborn as a Mule

The "Lynn McKenzie 'gag-and-hack' bit" is specially designed to bring hardheaded horses and mules under control. If horses could talk, they would probably call it a "torture bit." This bit is a two-part metal piece that goes in the horse's mouth. It is connected to a leather or rope bridle that goes over the horse's head. It has a steel bar that goes over its nose and positions the training bit in the animal's mouth. It is the "method of last resort" before an unruly stallion or horse goes to the "glue factory" or out to pasture. God has even more effective "training bits" for stubborn, rebellious, hardheaded, or "difficult to train" people who just have to learn things the hard way. The Psalmist knew all about these kinds of people:

> *Blessed is he whose transgression is forgiven, whose sin is covered. Blessed is the man unto whom the Lord imputeth not iniquity, and in whose spirit there is no guile. … I will instruct thee and teach thee in the way which thou shalt go: I will guide thee with Mine eye.* **Be ye not as the horse, or as the mule, which have no understanding: whose mouth must be held in with bit and bridle,** *lest they come near unto thee* (Psalm 32:1-2, 8-9).

Animal rights activists and animal lovers get upset about things like this, but many of these people have no problem using a "choker" collar on a large dog such as a German shepherd or a Doberman pinscher in public. Any experienced animal trainer or pet owner can tell you that rewards alone rarely do the trick when you are training animals with a stubborn streak. The problem with stubborn horses and mules is that they can easily get someone hurt or killed if their behavior isn't brought under control. If you are working with a stubborn horse or mule, then you have from 1,200 to 1,400 pounds worth of concentrated rebellion on your hands!

Horse trainers use the "Lynn McKenzie 'gag-and-hack' bit" because it works. It makes rebellion and disobedience so painful that after the training, most horses and mules *won't need that bit*. They quickly learn that obedience is better than pain, and many of them will obey even the lightest touch of the reins or a spoken command.

Basically, when a horse or hardheaded mule acts up, the rider pulls up on the reins and this "gag-and-hack" bit tightens up like a vise on the horse's mouth and nose. The top bar presses down on the horse's nose, the bottom strap or chain bites into the bottom ridges under the chin, and the bit inside the horse's mouth exerts painful pressure on the mouth, tongue, and gums. Disobedience brings pain and discomfort in three areas, along with a "gagging" feeling caused by a severe constriction of oxygen. This may seem like "overkill," but it is very important to stop nearly a ton of rampaging horse or mule. The moment the pressure is released on the reins, the pain stops. The developers of this unique training bit guarantee their product will train a horse, and for obvious reasons.

God used His own version of a "Lynn McKenzie 'gag-and-hack' bit" on a hardheaded young stallion named Saul of Tarsus (see Acts 9). This headstrong young rabbi was on his way down the road to persecute fellow Jews who followed Jesus when the Lord looked at him and said, "Hmmm. I'll need to use something special for this one." He looked around His tackle room for just the right bit and bridle. "This man has a serious problem—he's as stubborn as a mule. I think I'll just take care of him right away." That is when the Lord pulled out His patented "Holy Ghost 'gag and hack' bit" and slipped it right over Rabbi Saul's eyes and nose. Wham! Saul's mouth was slammed shut, his air supply was cut off, his nose went down, and he fell to the ground like he had been struck by lightning. For the first time, Saul acknowledged the Master he claimed was an impostor:

And he fell to the earth, and heard a voice saying unto him, Saul, Saul, why persecutest thou Me? And he said, Who art Thou, Lord? And the Lord said, I am Jesus whom thou persecutest: it is hard for thee to kick against the pricks. And he trembling and astonished said, Lord, what wilt Thou have me to do?... (Acts 9:4-6).

Saul was as stubborn as a mule. How about you? Has the Lord been trying to get your attention? Have you noticed that your life is beginning to fall apart around you? If so, your stubbornness may have earned you a training session with the "Holy Ghost 'gag-and-hack' bit." Are you feeling some sharp pricks to your heart? God probably has His spurs on! It looks like the Holy Spirit has jabbed you in what my kids call the "boo-hiney." God only uses the sharpest spurs at this stage because He wants to cure you of your rebellion so you can get on with your destiny in this life.

If God has faithfully jabbed your backside, prodded you, and urged you to reach out for more for this long, *are you moving yet?* He's done everything for you, friend. He's trying to be kind. He jabs, prods, convicts, and corrects you because He loves you, and He doesn't want your life to go to waste! He is saying, "Get going; get saved; get your family to the altar; get right with Me." He's tried everything else. Now if you are still as stubborn as a mule, there may be a bridle and bit in your future! Even worse, He may leave you to wallow in your own manure.

Let me give you a little clue about guidance, friend. Each of us has a choice. We can be led by God's "eye" as the Psalmist wrote, or we can be led around like a stupid, stubborn mule with a painful bit in our mouth and a restraining bridle wrapped around our bone-hard heads. "Be ye not as the horse, or as the mule, which have no understanding: whose mouth must be held in with bit and bridle, lest they come near unto thee" (Ps. 32:9). In simple English, that means, "Don't act like a stubborn mule." This message is so simple that it almost scares me. It leaves no room for excuses or explanations. When it comes to the things of God, are you stubborn, obstinate, unyielding, bullheaded, cantankerous, hardheaded, or headstrong? I've lost count of the times I heard people say in a baptismal pool, "God's been trying to get a hold of me for years." Every one of them regretted the 5, 10, or 20 years they wasted away from God's blessings and anointing. How about you? Friend, you are as stubborn as a mule!

I believe without a doubt that Jesus Christ has been trying to get hold of many of us. The Holy Spirit has been working on some of us for years through faithful pastors, lay leaders, and even through trials and tribulations! Some of the hard things you are going through right now were sent from God. Has your business crashed? It may be that God is trying to tell you something by pulling the plug on your life. Again, you have a choice. You can soften your heart and look to Heaven, or you can became even harder and more mulish, like Pharaoh did just before he was destroyed in the Red Sea (see Ex. 14).

Has God sent Christian witnesses your way to tell you how God can change your life? Did you shrug it off? Did God lead you to a Christian program on one of your more desperate nights, the night a Holy Ghost-anointed preacher pointed his finger at you and spoke the secrets of your heart? If you turned him off as well, then you are a master procrastinator. (You are really bucking for the title, "the master of disaster"!) You may tell yourself a thousand times, "Well, time is on my side. I'll get right with God some other day. It's just not convenient right now," but that doesn't make it so. I thought for sure that you could spot a lie when you heard one: Don't believe your own lies. It's time to get right with God. Your problem is that you are as stubborn as a mule.

Whether you are a Christian or a heathen right now, you read the words of God: "Be ye not as the horse, or as the mule, which have no understanding..." (Ps. 32:9). Basically, God is saying you are stupid and ignorant if you are stubborn. Don't be like that. The Holy Ghost is trying to get your attention so He can lead and guide you to all truth and joy. He wants to train you and make you into a prize stallion, but you're always bucking up against Him. Do you know what a mule is? A mule is a *hybrid*, a mix between a horse and a donkey. The males are bigger and stronger than horses or donkeys, *but they are all sterile*. Most of them are characterized by stubbornness. If you are mulish, then you are sterile, and you are always giving God lame excuses for your laziness and outright rebellion. This preacher is warning you in love: Do not be like the mule or a stubborn horse. It will only lead to a bit and bridle or worse.

How many times have you sat in a church service or heard someone's anointed testimony and felt God speak directly to your heart? How many times have you been hit by the "arrows of the Lord" that bring conviction and a deep desire to get right with God—and did nothing about it? Don't be like the stubborn mule or horse.

One of the favorite excuses the devil will add to your overused list is this: "I'm waiting until I understand more about this Christianity thing." Perhaps you creatively adapted this worn-out excuse to say, "I'm waiting until I understand more about this 'revival thing' before I get into it."

Friend, it will pass you by. Most of the mules who have been "waiting to understand" are dumber and colder than they were a year and a half ago! And two or three years from now, they'll be even dumber. I don't mean to make fun of anyone, but frankly, the choice is theirs. God doesn't bless doubt and unbelief. He knows the difference between honest concern and Spirit-led investigation of a thing, and old-fashioned stubbornness! Just when you think you have God "figured out" (translation: explained and controlled), He has moved on to something fresh and different.

In one revival service, God might reveal His presence with the physical sensation of a gentle breeze literally blowing through the auditorium. Then people might start falling to the floor all over the sanctuary just as they did at the dedication of the temple of Solomon in the Old Testament. I've seen sinners fall from their seats as if they were dead when the convicting presence of God fell on a revival meeting. First-time visitors have been so overcome that we had to carry them up front and drop them at the altar to get saved. Just when you think you have God figured out, friend, He will outgrow the box you've created with your limited, finite mind. So don't give me or the Lord the worn-out excuse, "I'm waiting until I understand more about this...."

If you're still acting like a mule (don't act offended; if the label doesn't apply, it won't stick), if you still say you want to understand before you "get in," then I have to tell you something. Get in, and then you'll understand. We are talking about the things of God. You are like a little baby who wants to be an adult *right now*—you don't want to start at childhood.

My little girl, Kelsey, is really enjoying being a kid. She doesn't gripe and complain because she "doesn't understand adulthood." She's having too much fun! My wonderful wife can clean our house and have it looking picture perfect, but in a matter of minutes our little girl can change that scene to a picture of chaos and devastation! Every parent knows what I'm talking about. If it has a handle or knob, Kelsey will grab it, pull it, jerk it, and empty it! Socks fly everywhere. Every tube of toothpaste is blessed with a squeeze—p-h-t-t-t! No, Kelsey doesn't have the time or the interest to gripe about "understanding adulthood." She's too busy exploring the wonders of growing up *today*, of facing *today's challenges* and learning *today's lessons* to worry about tomorrow. She is having a blast.

Friend, whether you are a Christian "checking out" the revival or a sinner at the brink of hell's gate, I urge you to throw away the arguments and excuses and just run to God's mercy! Get right with God first! Say "YES!" first. If you want to be convinced, then get converted. Run to Jesus first; then He will "convince you" He's real. "But I want to feel the love of God first. Then I'll get in." No, I'm telling you: Get in first, then you'll feel His love.

"Steve, I want God to speak to me in an audible voice. Then I'll be convinced of your sincerity." Friend, you've got it backwards. God is waiting for you to speak to Him in an audible voice. Then He'll be convinced of *your* sincerity. He proved His sincerity on a lonely cross at Calvary! Do not be a mule.

"Well, I'm waiting for the *perfect time*." What is the perfect time for you, friend? Is it at the brink of divorce? What is the perfect time for you to give your life to Jesus? Do you need to suffer through a near-fatal car wreck first? Are you waiting for the death of a loved one before you will run to God? Are you waiting for financial collapse before you collapse at God's feet? God is speaking to your heart right now. When will you answer Him?

While we are stalling around and making excuses, there are other people watching us and depending on us for leadership in their lives. Parents who say, "We're waiting for the *perfect time* to come to God" might as well be saying, "We're waiting until our procrastination produces tragedy before we will answer God's call. We'll call out His name when our sons and daughters are on drugs and our marriage is on the rocks." That is hogwash. There is no "perfect time" tomorrow—*now is the time*, friend! If you don't know Jesus Christ, then *today* is your day of salvation! Today is your day of obedience to the call of God, Christian friend.

If you are saying, "There's just too much to give up right now," or "I'm waiting until I find a group of perfect Christians that I can be a part of," then you have a serious problem of "mule-itis." You say, "I'm waiting for my friends and family to make a commitment." What a lousy excuse. They're probably waiting for you! Quit acting like a mule. God is trying to get your attention and that is why everything is falling apart. All He is trying to do is get you to repent of your sins and live for Him.

I used to train a Tennessee Walking horse named "Sonny" inside a training ring. The training gear consisted of a halter, a rope, and a leader. I would just lead Sonny around that little ring and then move to the center while Sonny continued around the ring with the most beautiful canter you'd ever see. I loved training Sonny—until I stepped into the saddle and left the barn and training ring.

As long as I rode away from the stable, we were fine. But once I turned Sonny back toward that barn, that stubborn horse made up his mind he was headed back to the barn, his oats, his wheat, his water trough, and his comfortable straw-lined bed. It didn't matter what I had planned for that day. Sonny was what horse trainers call "barn sour." Unfortunately, "barn sour Christians" who are drawn away from their muddy pens by revival do okay for awhile. But as soon as they get a glimpse of their old life with its carnal pleasures, they are drawn back to their carnal barn and no longer care about God's agenda for their lives.

Jesus said, "No man, having put his hand to the plough, and looking back, is fit for the kingdom of God" (Lk. 9:62b). Stubborn mules (the human variety) get lots of "help" from the enemy of their souls. The devil will show up at exactly the wrong moment and whisper, "Here, take this pornography. Take this music. Come on, eat of these carnal delights. Fill your flesh. Get fat." The devil is fattening you up like a farmer would fatten up a pig for slaughter. He's separated you by your choices, and now he's got you. It doesn't pay to be a stubborn "barn sour" Christian.

Christian, are you acting like "a calf at a new gate"? Are you afraid of the "new thing" the Lord is trying to do in your life? Have you refused to pass through His gate to a higher and deeper level of obedience? He is doing a new thing, and He wants you and me involved. But He has no use for stubborn mules and horses. Don't be a mule, friend.

The best trained horses in the world are either "neck-reined" or require no bridle at all! American plains Indians and certain people in ancient Europe and Asia trained horses for battle to respond to the subtlest shifts of their master's weight instantly—without reins, bridles, bits, or even saddles in some cases. Today, modern horsemen want their horses to respond instantly to delicate touches of the reins on the necks of their horses. These splendid animals don't require harsh commands or acts of force; they obey instantly because they want to please their masters. God wants even more than that. He is looking for sons and daughters who will respond to His slightest glance with instant, joyful obedience—*because they love Him.*

Don't be stubborn like a mule, friend. Yield to His touch and be willing to go where He wants you to go.

God is flooding this world with His presence in a world-changing revival right now. He is pretty sick and tired of wasting so much time on stubborn mules who refuse to respond or obey when so many lost and hurting souls are crying out for a Savior. My friend, the day may come when He will put away His bridle. He will remove his "Holy Ghost 'gag-and-hack' bit" and turn you out to that hellish pasture you think is so much better than Heaven. If that happens, you can take that as a clear sign that you're good for nothing, friend. If God finally lets you go, there's no one else left to pick up the pieces. Have you ever met people who don't feel the presence of God anymore? They are hollow shells of what they once were. Why? Because their loving Trainer finally left them to their own devices. They chose to be untrainable, so now they have been cut loose from their destiny. These people truly "have no future."

God is more than just a merciful God. He is also totally just. Justice means you get what you deserve. God has already been offering you something *better* than what you deserve for a whole lifetime. How close are you to "getting your own way"? If I were you, I sure wouldn't want to get *what I deserve*. God warned us in the Bible that He would not contend or wrestle with us forever (see Is. 57:16). His Spirit will not always deal with you. Right now, you can still sense God speaking to you. Don't make Him bring out the painful training bit. Don't make the stubborn choices that will put you in a lonely pasture and a burning hell for eternity. Just say, "Jesus, I'm tired of fighting You. I am yielding to You tonight, Lord. I turn my life over to You tonight."

If you have wandered away from God, He is saying to you right now, "Quit acting like a mule. Be the child of God I created you to be. You know My voice because you can hear it right now. Come to Me when I call to you. Quit being so stubborn." He is speaking to you, and if you're away from God as you read these words, then this is your time to change directions. Ask Him to forgive you for the sin in your life. The reason you can feel His presence right now is because He wants you to run to Him.

Jesus Christ died on the cross 2,000 years ago for you. He shed His blood on Calvary for you. The only thing He left behind on the face of this earth was His blood, and He shed that blood for you. He hung nude on Calvary's cross to take the blame and punishment you deserve for your sin—and He was totally innocent. He did it for you because He loves you. Long before I ever thought about preaching this message or writing this book, Jesus Christ looked past the cross and saw you pick up this book. He watched you begin to read the words on these pages. He saw you reading this book right where you are today! When He said, "Father, forgive them; for they know not what they do" (Lk. 23:34b), He was also saying, "Father, forgive Sally, for she knows not what she does. Forgive Jim, for he knows not what he does. Forgive Judy, for she knows not what she does."

He saw you standing at the cross of decision today when He spoke your name to the Father in that prayer 2,000 years ago! He knew you and loved you before you were born, friend. That is why He let sinful men spit on Him, beat Him, and hang Him on that cross. Now it's your turn. You know the truth about what He did for you. What are you going to do for Him? All of Heaven is watching. Don't even think about standing before God on Judgment Day to give Him an excuse for passing this opportunity by! He won't be interested in anything you have to say—unless you say, "I received Jesus Christ as my Lord and Savior." Are you listening?

Christian, if there is secret sin in your life that is separating you from your God right now, you need to answer His call to holiness. You already know that God doesn't have time or patience with excuses. No lie is good enough on Judgment Day; you will be mute. You will only be able to fall on your face and cry out, "My Lord and my God, have mercy." I fear that some of us will hear Him say, "Depart from Me; I don't even know you. You were ashamed of Me before men. You didn't have the courage to declare My name to your friends, even though I hung on the cross in public humiliation and shame in your place."

Come to the Lord right now, right where you are, and pray out loud to God, "Jesus, I surrender *all*. It's over. I will be obedient to You from this point on. I am sorry for all my sins and rebellion. I am Yours from this moment on, Lord Jesus. My stubborn days are over. I'm giving my life to You one hundred percent."

I'll never forget the day I yielded my life to Jesus. It was on Tuesday, October 28, 1975, at 11 o'clock in the morning. From that day on, I made up my mind I would go where He led me. *What are you waiting on?* You just read about the dangers of being "as stubborn as a mule." Why are you hesitating and thinking, "Well, I don't know. I just don't know." You're acting like a mule again, friend. Some of the most stubborn people on this planet are men. He will put you out to pasture if you keep ignoring His call. You can turn it around right now by giving your life to God. Your life is being weighed in the balance. You are letting your appetite for sin and stubborn rebellion outweigh His call to eternal life. The worst thing that can happen is that you get what you are pushing for: life apart from God. That is the best definition for hell that I know of. All you have to remember is that eternity apart from God means eternity in the flames and the eternal torment of hell. Give that secret sin to Jesus right now before it destroys you.

An 18-year-old boy who seemed to be a fine Christian came to me after a revival service and confessed that he had been eaten alive by pornography for seven years. He had been in the church the whole time, but he didn't know God. That kid came forward because someone dared to ask him, "Do you need forgiveness?" I'm asking you right now, "Do you need forgiveness?"

Are you like a hard-to-train horse—are you stubborn? Do you wait and procrastinate on everything? You will damn your soul waiting around like that. Listen, when God speaks, you move. Why should He have to speak to you 18 times? Why does God have to allow problems to consume your life just to get your attention? Just yield to Him and reap the eternal benefits of life and joy in Jesus. If you have fallen into temptation and sin, you need to turn from it and walk away right now. Don't procrastinate. Come to Jesus *right now*. Pray this prayer out loud:

Dear Jesus, thank You for speaking to my heart. Thank You for not leaving me alone. I don't want to be stubborn anymore. I want to confess that I have sinned against You, Lord Jesus, and I have hurt others. I repent and ask for Your forgiveness. Wash my sins away. Thank You for dying for me on Calvary 2,000 years ago. I receive Your forgiveness, and I ask You to be my Savior, my Lord, and my very best friend. From this moment on, I am Yours and You are mine. I pray this in Jesus' name. Amen.

Chapter 4

Pig's Feet and Dog's Vomit

"Let the dogs bark; the caravan is moving on."

Pastor Carey Robertson was talking about *revival* when he said these words. Well, I'm not calling you a dog, friend, but if you don't like revival, then you need to step aside. Jesus was even more direct. In Matthew 7, He warned His disciples not to judge others, and in verse 6, He said something that is shocking even in our day: "Give not that which is holy unto the dogs, neither cast ye your pearls before swine, lest they trample them under their feet, and turn again and rend [lacerate or tear] you."

I agree with the Bible expositors and commentators who say Jesus was not forbidding His disciples to preach the gospel to wicked or heathen people. Jesus Himself often preached to publicans and sinners. He said, "It's not those who are well who need a physician, but those who are sick" (see Mt. 9:12). Jesus was talking about scoffers, skeptics, critics, and naysayers dressed in religious costumes and bound up in religious ritual and self-righteousness.

God wants to share something precious with you because He loves you! The Lord has a pocket full of precious pearls, and He has one for you. He has intended to bless you from the beginning. Whether you are young or old, married or single, or white, black, brown, or red, God wants to bless you. He has a plan for your life—even if you are pushing 85 and think your life is about over.

Jesus said, "Give not that which is holy unto the dogs, neither cast ye your pearls before swine" (Mt. 7:6a). Jesus was saying we should never surrender the higher to the lower. Never submit the celestial to the terrestrial. Never desecrate the consecrated. Jesus was painting a picture for His disciples and a mostly Jewish crowd on the side of a mountain. That picture was plainly understood by every Jew who heard His words. They pictured a priest or a Levite leaving the temple after completing his duty shift, who encountered a coarse, ravenous dog at the temple gate. The dog was like hundreds of others that roamed the streets of Jerusalem. When the priest noticed the dog's pitiful "help me, I'm dying" look, he returned to the remains of the burnt sacrifice in the outer court and carefully looked to make sure no one was watching. Then the priest ripped off a fleshy portion of the holy sacrifice and threw it out to the dog outside the gate! The priest had just violated the divine law by giving to a dog the flesh of the burnt sacrifice specifically reserved for priests and their families alone. His action demonstrated a gross disrespect for the holy things of God. Every Jew who heard the Lord's warning would think, "Giving the holy sacrifice to the dogs? Come on!"

The Lord painted a second picture about judgment that was just as distasteful to observant Jews. It involved precious pearls as well as the most despised symbol of defilement in Jewish culture: a pig. Jesus' words painted a picture of a rich man who was so wealthy that he casually cast precious pearls to swine as if they were seed or food. The pigs of Palestine were not tame like domesticated pigs in the United States. They would snort up to the pearls like wary wild animals anticipating a meal. When they smelled the pearls and sensed the deception, they were likely to trample the pearls in the muck and mire of their wallow and then bore into their deceiver in rage, like wild animals attacking prey.

Jesus said, "Give not that which is holy unto the dogs, neither cast ye your pearls before swine" (Mt. 7:6a). I am sharing something holy and precious with you. I am casting pearls to you as I preach this message. With each word I pull another priceless bead from my pocket and toss it.

"Jesus loves you. He has a plan for your life. Jesus can heal you. He can heal your backslidings. He *can* set you free!" These are the pearls I throw out to you, friend.

What are you going to do with the Word of God? You can trample His pearls under foot like a pig or you can be like the man Jesus described who sold all he had just to purchase a pearl of great price (see Mt. 13:45-46). Jesus is the pearl of great price. He is the Lamb of God who takes away the sin of the world (see Jn. 1:29). He is the sacrificial Lamb who fulfilled the Law and the Prophets. He is the One who died for you and me on Mount Calvary. He is the One who paid the price for you, friend. He is the One whom God...

> *...hath highly exalted...and given Him a name which is above every name: that at the name of Jesus every knee should bow, of things in heaven, and things in earth, and things under the earth; and that every tongue should confess that Jesus Christ is Lord, to the glory of God the Father* (Philippians 2:9-11).

It's amazing to see how things in the natural often mirror realities in the supernatural. *The same sun that melts ice hardens clay.* It's up to you whether you want to be a pig, a dog, or a lamb when God tosses you a pearl. You can receive the Word of God or you can snort at it in disgust. You can whine like a dog and bargain for a *portion* of God's plan for your life, or you can be a lamb and say, "Yes, baaaah, I want all You have for me, Lord Jesus. I give my all to You, Lord. I'll serve you always, Lord. Pour out Your Spirit on me!" It's up to you, friend.

Some people come to this revival with hearts as hard as rock. They have no intention of yielding to the Holy Ghost. At first, they sit in their seat like cold hunks of coal. They refuse to budge as the Spirit lifts the congregation to the heavenlies in worship. Then something happens—many people finally crack during our Friday night baptismal services, when people from all walks of life testify about their deliverance from drugs, depression, or witchcraft.

It might begin with a lady's story of how she was abused as a child and carried that pain all her life. The last of the hardness in some listeners may fall away as the woman tells how Jesus came and washed away all that pain, since testimonies of God's goodness are like rain falling on hardened hearts. I've watched it thousands of times. By the time the preacher comes out, the man or woman who was hard as a rock is now saying, "I hope this never ends." I love to toss pearls of hope out there to hardened souls, and see them catch hold of God's treasures. Now His pearls are precious to them. When the altar call is given, they run to meet God on their knees.

On the other hand, some people stay hard and bitter all the way through the service, muttering, "I ain't gonna listen to this. That preacher is either calling me a pig or a dog. I'm not gonna take it. Who does he think he is to talk about sin and unrighteousness like that? Does he think he's holier than me? He doesn't know God any better than I do!"

I don't mean to offend you with this image, but "picking and choosing" what you will accept and reject from God is like ripping off a limb of Jesus or ripping off a part of His sacrifice on Calvary! His whole body was bruised, beaten, whipped, and pierced for you. A thorny crown was forced onto His head—all according to God's divine plan. God doesn't want anyone asking some preacher, "Give me just a little portion of Jesus. Throw me a little leg from the sacrificial Lamb while I wait outside the temple gate. I don't want to come *all the way in*." May God have mercy on your soul, friend.

Dogs are notorious for returning to their own vomit. They can get sick from eating tainted food and vomit, and then turn right back to that mess again. Wild dogs and dogs without masters are the worst because they never settle down under authority where they eat a balanced, healthy diet. They live on scraps, tainted and decaying food, and wild game. They have no Master to set food before them.

Don't come to the Lamb of God who takes away the sin of the world and try to bargain for your advantage. "Lord, You can have my family problems and my financial problems, and I'll even throw in my nervous condition if you will let me keep my pride and my little pornography problem. I'll let You in, but I'm not going to give up my 'freedom' to live in Your house. I may want to return to my favorite sin [vomit] again." You need to look at Jesus in His entirety. He gave His all, and He demands your all—without apology.

One time I held a severed pig's foot right in the middle of this message. Can you see it in your mind's eye? I don't want you to forget this message as long as you live. That is how serious it is. I can almost hear the snorting pigs and whimpering dogs throughout the world and the church today. Has God been working on you for years? Have preachers cast holy pearls to you, loved and cared for you, only to be trampled by hoofed pigs' feet?

You've heard the Word, you know the truth, and you know the truth can set you free—if you don't trample it. Yes, even Christians can trample the pearls of God! Holiness is a pearl of God. Totally living for God is a pearl of the Kingdom. If you are offended by the Lord's demand for a holy life, then you are trampling on His Word. You are trampling

God's Word in the muck if you stomp out of church saying, "Preacher, I don't want to hear any more of that stuff on tithing or offerings. Back off from that talk about a holy life. Quit talking about sin."

How many times have you had "roast preacher" at the restaurant after a church service? You not only trample the pearls of God's Word underfoot, but you also turn and "rend" or tear at the vessel who delivered the Word! If you are offended right now, I'm throwing in front of you the very thing that you need! Jesus loves you and has a plan for your life, friend. Don't stomp all over it like an angry pig in a pigsty. The Lord said, "Be ye holy; for I am holy" (1 Pet. 1:16). Take that pearl and guard it with your life.

Many of us are surrounded by mounds of mud-covered pearls. We just keep on stomping on everything that Jesus has been trying to do in our lives. How long has God been trying to speak to you and deliver you? Has He been trying to heal your marriage while you continually trample all over Him? Are there pearls stuck between your hoofed feet, my friend? Don't get riled with me; just get right with God. Are you angry with God because you don't have your healing or because your marriage isn't healed? If you don't watch it, you will stomp over the very thing that could heal you!

The beautiful thing about God is that He can change a pig into a gentle lamb! He also transforms barking, yelping, and whining dogs into gentle lambs. As soon as the Holy Ghost begins to move, things begin to change. Old things become new right in front of your eyes. Before you know it, the dog begging for flesh has disappeared and a lamb seeking the pearls of God appears.

I can't tell you how many times I've watched "mean old dogs" come into a revival service and go out singing, "Yes, Jesus loves me, for the Bible tells me so." Too many of us want Jesus as Savior, but we don't want Him as Lord. "I don't want to live the sacrificed life just now, but I want to be healed of cancer right now, Jesus." That is just as twisted as ripping off pieces of the burnt sacrifice! It desecrates what is holy.

God has been wooing you home night after night. Every day God finds new ways to tell you He loves you and has a plan for your life, but the Holy Spirit also convicts you of sin. He convicts you of sin because sin separates you from God. When the Holy Ghost shows up in your life, that's a pearl, friend. If you trample it, then you are being obstinate and rebellious. How long do you think God is going to put up with that?

Don't talk to me about the so-called "permissive will of God." That is a hoax. There is the will of God, and there is the will of the flesh. The only time the will of the flesh is good is when it is in line with the will of God. Period. One man who was involved in an adulterous affair said, "God understands what I'm going through." I said, "Yeah, He understands you are in sin. If you don't repent, you are going to go to hell." He said, "No, that's not what I'm saying. He knows how my wife and I don't get along together." I said, "Sir, I repeat, you are in sin. If you don't repent, you're going to hell."

Jesus came down to this earth and lived a holy life as a man to show us that we can live holy too! You can turn away from that "other" woman. You can turn away from the pornography, the drugs, and the alcoholism. You can turn away from the hate, the bitterness, and the strife and live a victorious life for God—but you have to do it His way, not yours.

I love the old versions of Webster's Dictionary dating from around 1840 or 1850. Noah Webster defined "conviction" this way: "to be found guilty, as in the conviction of the Holy Ghost," and he added a Scripture for good measure. The entire dictionary is full of Scripture! He defined the word, "walk" as: "to move one leg in front of the other as in to walk with God, to walk for God, to walk after the Spirit, to walk in the things of the Spirit, to walk after the flesh." Webster said, "Conviction is to be found guilty as in the conviction of the Holy Ghost." That means you are *convicted* if the Holy Ghost is saying to you, "You're the one. You're the one." We have all been convicted of a crime. We are ex-convicts who were guilty of a crime. Jesus came to pardon and forgive.

If there is sin in your life, you need to do something about it right now. The only thing that will keep you from experiencing forgiveness is your pride, and pride is an abomination to God. The Bible says God resists the proud and loves the humble (see Jas. 4:6). If you have pride hidden in your heart, it will damn your soul, friend. You know you need to get forgiveness. Have you trampled the Word of God? The Bible says God is ready and able to make you brand-new, but you will have to take a step toward Him. "Therefore if any man be in Christ, he is a new creature: old things are passed away; behold, all things are become new" (2 Cor. 5:17). He will transform you, friend. But you're going to have to make the next move. God has already moved Heaven and earth for you.

I'll never forget the day a preacher came to 514 Pearson Drive in Huntsville, Alabama, and stuck a pearl in front of my face. For years, I was just a "snortin' pig and a barkin' dog." Then came the day everything changed—the day the preacher held that pearl in front of me. He said, "Steve, Jesus loves you and He has a plan for your life." I reached out and grabbed that pearl and held it to my chest. I called out to Jesus and my life has never been the same! He made me brand-new, friend.

If you need the Lord, if you need to ask Jesus Christ to forgive you, friend, then do it *now*. Don't say, "Well, I'll deal with this tomorrow." That simply means you don't have the courage to deal with your sin today. When tomorrow rolls around, you may actually kneel by your bedside and sputter out your three-second prayer to God. But do you want to know what you will hear by your bedside, friend? You are going to hear these words:

> *"Just a few hours ago, My Spirit stirred your heart as you read a book on revival. My servant gave you a pearl and asked you to act by faith and call upon My name. Are you ashamed of Me? My Son hung on the cross nude for you 2,000 years ago. He bled and died for you. He was whipped, beaten, spat upon, cursed, smitten, crowned with thorns, and nailed to a cross for you. He walked as a man 33-and-a-half years on the face of the earth for you. For you! He walked Calvary's road to His own death. He was crucified on Calvary for all to see. Why couldn't you take one step to receive Jesus, My pearl of great price, and ask for forgiveness of sin?"*

Think about it, friend. How do you think God looks at your pride? If you want to receive Jesus, then you must be willing to follow the Good Shepherd wherever He goes. In return He will give you precious truths, eternal forgiveness, new life, hope, peace, and joy. If it seems God hasn't been at work in your life, it might be because you have always put Him off. Do you know Jesus? Do you wake up in the morning with Jesus on your heart? Do you go to sleep at night with Jesus on your heart? If you don't, friend, I question whether you know Him, for you're supposed to be a bride. You're supposed to be the Bride of Christ awaiting the Groom.

If there is one person reading these words who is going to hell, then I'm not satisfied. There is freedom in Jesus Christ, friend. Outside of Christ, hell itself awaits you. Just beyond the door of His Kingdom, lucifer is waiting, along with every chain and every form of bondage he can muster. If there is sin in your life, I urge you to be a man or a woman and say, "Yes, I need forgiveness, Lord Jesus." I don't care if you are the pastor of the largest church in your town—please don't lie to the Holy Spirit like Ananias and Sapphira in Acts 5:1-11. As you read these words inspired by the Holy Spirit of God, you will sense the presence of God Himself in this place. The very place where you are right now is holy ground. It's time to take care of God's business. When Jesus gave His life on the cross, He paid the highest price to set you free from sin. It is time to honor Him for His sacrifice by giving Him your life—all of it.

Whether you walk with God, or have wandered far from Him, the Lord is in charge of the harvest. He knows what is going on in your life and in the lives of those you love. It is no accident that you are reading these words right now. A woman from Minneapolis who was involved in white witchcraft showed up at a revival service. She looked like she had just stepped out of a fashion magazine. All the way through the altar call, she stood in the back of the room. She wouldn't budge until somebody turned to her and said, "Do you need Jesus Christ to forgive you?" That was the first time anybody had ever confronted her with the gospel one on one. She made her way down to the altar and God transformed her life! The same thing happened to a drug dealer from Hattiesburg, Mississippi. He stonewalled his way through the entire altar call; but when somebody cared enough to ask him, "Do you need Jesus Christ to forgive you?" he surrendered his life to Jesus Christ and was set free forever!

It is no accident that this book ended up in your hands. Either you are supposed to respond and receive Christ right now, or you are supposed to be asking other people around you, "Do you need Jesus Christ to forgive you?" Have you been making the same mistake I did one night by making assumptions? I saw a man decked out in an $800 suit, and based on his appearance I automatically assumed he was a godly man. I went down to him to talk with him and he cut me off in a heartbeat! He looked at me and said, "Look at me, sir. I'm an adulterer and a pornographer." That man looked clean, smelled clean, and walked clean in that meeting, but he was a pornographer living in sin, friend. He just didn't look like what I thought he should look like if he was going to be involved in all the stuff he was involved in. If you are saved, you have an obligation to care enough about others to lay aside your assumptions and ask them point blank, "Do you need Jesus Christ to forgive you?" You could save their souls from eternal damnation by asking one question in love.

I love tears of repentance, and I love to hear folks publicly give their lives to Jesus and repent of their sin. But the true test of an evangelist's work and of any commitment to God comes ten years from now. What will your life demonstrate in the year 2007? Will you still be burning white hot for Jesus Christ, or will you still be flirting with damnation by living the lukewarm life free of commitment, truth, and sacrifice? If you know the Holy Ghost is speaking to your heart right now, then you need to do something about. I want you to bow your head and pray this prayer with me right now, right where you are:

Dear Jesus, thank You for speaking to my heart. Thank You for not leaving me alone. I ask You right now to forgive me because I have sinned against You and I've hurt others. I ask You to be my Savior, my Lord, and my very best friend right now. I give myself to You one hundred percent. From this moment on, I am Yours and You are mine. In Jesus' name. Amen.

Chapter 5

The Rebel's Reward

One morning when I got up to hear from the Lord, He took me to the story of Saul's disobedience to God. I had never preached an evangelical message on that passage, although I had referred to it many times. As I began to study Saul's rebellion, I felt the heat of the devil's breath on my back!

It felt like lucifer himself was peering over my shoulder and breathing down my neck. I could sense an evil presence saying, "Don't you dare talk on the subject of rebellion. I will come against you as never before. I will take away your train of thought and bring a spirit of despondency upon the congregation! I'll cause confusion and launch waves of warfare against you if you preach on Saul's rebellion."

Then the arch liar took a different approach. "Besides that, Steve [I haven't been on a first-name basis with satan since I was saved!], you are tired. Just relax during the revival service tonight and calm down. There is no urgency. You can always share on this subject 'some other time.'"

Friend, I can honestly say that I really appreciated lucifer's encouraging words. God used him to inspire a life-changing message, and I praise God for it. When the devil tries so hard to discourage me from preaching a God-sent, God-inspired, soul-convicting message from the Holy Ghost—*it has to be good*! If the archangel of rebellion goes to all the trouble to try to "calm me down," then I know I'm supposed to preach that message with everything I've got! Anything that riles the devil will bless God!

I take every opportunity I can get to jar the adversary in the teeth. I'd just like to say, "Thank you, devil, for your attention that morning. Your words were just the boost I needed to go forward with this message. I would also like to proclaim that you are a liar and the father of all lies. The Word of God says there is no truth in you." If you are a pastor and a "word" comes to you from somewhere that there will be no revival in your church, write it down and underline it. Revival is on its way!

The devil's negative comments that morning were all lies. He was discouraged because he knew what God was encouraging. Any time the father of lies hisses, "No one will respond, preacher," I know exactly what needs to be preached! This message, which I call "The Rebel's Reward," may be difficult for you. It is about "getting what you deserve." It might be so be hard to swallow that you could gag on it. If God is trying to speak to your heart through this message, then you *need to do something about it.*

First Samuel 15 describes how Saul, the newly anointed king of Israel, disobeyed God's command to destroy the Amalekites and everything that belonged to them:

And Samuel said, What meaneth then this bleating of the sheep in mine ears, and the lowing of the oxen which I hear? And Saul said, They have brought them from the Amalekites: for the people spared the best of the sheep and of the oxen, to sacrifice unto the Lord thy God; and the rest we have utterly destroyed. ... [Samuel said] Wherefore then didst thou not obey the voice of the Lord, but didst fly upon the spoil, and didst evil in the sight of the Lord? And Saul said...the people took of the spoil, sheep and oxen, the chief of the things which should have been utterly destroyed, to sacrifice unto the Lord thy God in Gilgal (1 Samuel 15:14-15, 19-21).

Saul bragged, "Hey, I have obeyed the voice of the Lord! I did what the Lord sent me to do, and I've even brought back Agag the king of Amalek as a trophy after we completely destroyed the Amalekites." He didn't know that God had already told Samuel the prophet that Saul had disobeyed His commands. Samuel lost a night's sleep over it and he wasn't in any mood to mess with Saul's lies. He asked Saul, "What then is this bleating of sheep in my ears?" God had commanded Saul to destroy *everything*. Samuel should have heard only silence.

Saul, like Adam in the Book of Genesis, blamed someone else for his own sin: "But *the people* took of the spoil, sheep and oxen, the chief of the things which *should have been* utterly destroyed..." (1 Sam. 15:21). Samuel answered Saul's excuse with a prophetic statement:

And Samuel said, Hath the Lord as great delight in burnt offerings and sacrifices, as in obeying the voice of the Lord? Behold, to obey is better than sacrifice, and to hearken than the fat of rams. For rebellion is as the sin of witchcraft, and stubbornness is as iniquity and idolatry. Because thou hast rejected the word of the Lord, He hath also rejected thee from being king (1 Samuel 15:22-23).

In God's eyes, your rebellion looks, feels, and smells like witchcraft and idolatry. Rebellion is "opposition to one in authority or dominance"[1] or an open and avowed renunciation of the authority of the government to which one owes allegiance. Rebellion is resisting the authority over you. When a parent tells me, "I have a rebellious son," I know that son doesn't obey. He is obstinate, and he bucks up against authority and accountability. Rebels defy authority. They are disobedient and insubordinate. Rebels revolt, trigger uprisings, are disloyal and mutinous, and are resistant and seditious. They are treasonable, ungovernable, and unruly. Are you rebellious?

God has done everything He can do for you. Are you still bucking up against Him? I'm talking directly to you, whether you are a sinner, pastor, layman, missionary, backslider, or Sunday school teacher! "Rebel" generally refers to someone "inside" an organization who defies proper order. I'm talking to you as a member of God's Kingdom, government, and household—or as someone God is talking to. Sinner, God will pass you by if you rebel against Him! Christian, you and your little group are not "God's plan" for this planet. He might just use the Episcopalian down the road, or pour out His Holy Spirit on a bunch of people who don't even have a church yet!

A rebellious spirit has woven itself into the fabric of this nation and the church! Has it woven itself into your life? Has God been trying to get your attention? Has He been whispering to you in the night hours? Did you answer, or are you rebellious? Don't get upset with me; God ordained that you would read these words at this moment.

An enemy owes no allegiance to the government he attacks. An enemy is not a rebel. Rebels in the church disobey God's will. Nothing provokes God's wrath like rebellion and disobedience. You are a rebel if you have set up your will in competition with His and said, "I'm going to do it my way." When you bowed your knee to Jesus Christ, He became Lord. The greatest thing that happened to me other than salvation was the realization, *I am not in charge anymore.*

Jesus Christ is Lord; He knows what is going to happen tomorrow. You have received Him as Lord of your life. Now live like it. You may be fidgeting right now because every force in hell wants you to put this book down and find something else to do to distract you from this message. The problem is that you know God put this book in your hands for an eternal reason. You know you are nailed. God has a plan for you, friend, and stubbornness will stop it cold. The word *stubbornness* has to do with inflexibility, fixed opinions, and an unwillingness to be moved or persuaded by reason. The word *obstinate* is often substituted for "stubborn." Almost 300 years ago, the philosopher John Locke said that "stubbornness and obstinate disobedience must be mastered with blows." (I'm sure he wasn't just talking about dealing with children.)

Sometimes God uses His Word like a "Holy Ghost two-by-four" to master our stubborn and obstinate disobedience with blows. He did it to Saul of Tarsus on the road to Damascus in Acts 9, and He got the attention of Charles Finney too. Finney was at home having devotions when suddenly he felt something like lightning sweep through his body. I believe the Lord was just getting Finney's attention because God was about to shake America through him. Maybe Brother Charles had a little stubbornness in him; I don't know. If Mr. Finney was the least bit stubborn, or if he thought he had a better plan, you can be sure God got rid of it before launching His nineteenth century awakenings. (Nothing works better than a little lightning from Heaven.)

King Saul's life makes most of us pity him. He wasn't some tyrant who made himself king and ruled the people against their will. The Bible tells us Saul was a choice young man with a striking personality who belonged to a wealthy and powerful family. He was chosen by God Himself and anointed by God's prophet to became Israel's first king at the express desire of the people. He was a brave and noble man. He led the Israelites against their enemies and by God's help was victorious over them. But there were also some terrible blots in his character. Everything goes back to his first great sin against God: his disobedience with the Amalekites.

Saul's jealous persecution of David was nothing more than wicked cruelty. Even so, we can't help but pity this man who had such potential but who lived such a sad and unhappy life. The root of his problem and his unhappy life can be summed up in one word: *rebellion.*

The words spoken by Samuel the prophet contain a lesson that Saul never learned. All who read these words need to learn from Saul and let his mistakes be a springboard for their advancement in the Kingdom of God (including you). Saul served God and he appeared to be zealous in God's cause, but he insisted on doing it in a way that suited his own pleasure and purposes. He served God as long as things were working out well for him. Whenever Saul's will had to be denied in favor of God's will, he rebelled. I'm speaking to some backsliders right now. Do things go well as long as they "go your way"? What happens when you "lose the feeling"? I pray that the "feelings" fall away from you, for I want you to be a soldier and warrior, not a baby or a spiritual invalid. I am asking God to raise up some Holy Ghost Green Berets who are ready for service and don't care whether they feel like going to war or not!

What do you do when things don't work out the way you want them to, or when God doesn't answer your prayers as quickly as you think He should? What happened when you found out that everybody wouldn't come to Jesus overnight like you wanted them to, or when you no longer felt the same excitement you felt the first time you got saved? Did you backslide? If you did, you are a spiritual wimp, friend. Don't walk around telling people, "I'm a Christian. I'm just not right with God right now." Tell them the truth. Say, "I'm a heathen." Otherwise you will confuse everybody. Tell them, "I'm a heathen. I'm as bad as a street junkie. I don't know God. I'm away from God because I am rebellious."

This isn't very pleasant, is it? Do you realize that Saul never really worshiped God at all? He was actually worshiping "self." He never learned the great truth that obedience to

God is the only thing pleasing in His eyes. I was privileged to spend several years with Leonard Ravenhill before he died, and I loved that dear man of God. *Obedience* was his favorite word. He would say, "Pour it all in a funnel—everything that is going on all over the world, pour it all in a funnel. The only thing that needs to come out of the bottom of that spout is obedience. Obey God. Do what He tells you to do."

Saul's life is a sad picture of those in our day who profess to be Christians and act "in a measure" as Christians. They talk the talk, but in reality they follow their own ways just as if they were under no Christian vows at all. They have never learned how to obey. Obedience to God requires self-denial and self-discipline. These qualities do not please the flesh.

The Book of First Samuel clearly shows that God told Saul exactly what He wanted him to do. He said, "Now go and smite Amalek, and utterly destroy *all that they have*, and spare them not; but slay both man and woman, infant and suckling, ox and sheep, camel and ass" (1 Sam. 15:3). Do you know what that meant? It meant "go and smite Amalek, and utterly destroy *all*." Some of us are more dense than others, so I am careful to repeat things that may seem obvious to some. The Bible is so clear. God says, "Honor Me; I'll honor you. Draw close to Me; I'll draw close to you. Resist the devil; he will flee" (see 1 Sam. 2:30, Jas. 4:8a, 7b). God's commands are straightforward and clear, like an equation: one plus one equals two. God's simple commands to Saul were crystal clear. The Amalekites, like the inhabitants of Jericho, were to be entirely devoted to destruction. Saul's personal feelings and reasoning were beside the point. God said go and destroy and He meant go and destroy.

Let me make this more personal. If you have received Jesus Christ as Lord and Savior, then God has told you exactly what to do: "That if thou shalt confess with thy mouth the Lord Jesus, and shalt believe in thine heart that God hath raised Him from the dead, thou shalt be saved" (Rom. 10:9). He said, "...Thou shalt love the Lord thy God with all thy heart, and with all thy soul, and with all thy mind" (Mt. 22:37). The Scriptures are filled with simple and direct commands. "Do this and I will bless you." You don't have to tell God, "I don't understand this." Mark Twain said "It is not the scriptures I don't understand that bother me; it is the scriptures I do understand that bother me."

From Genesis through the Book of Revelation, the Bible says, "Repent." If you say, "What do you want me to do with my pornographic problem, God?" His Word has the answer: Repent. "What do you want me to do with my adulterous lifestyle?" Repent. "My mouth is so vile and vulgar, what do you want me to do, God?" Repent. The Bible is incredibly clear when it says, "If My people, which are called by My name, shall humble themselves, and pray, and seek My face, and turn from their wicked ways; then will I hear from heaven..." (2 Chron. 7:14). In First Thessalonians 5:22, Paul told us to "abstain from all appearance of evil." That means you should "abstain from all appearance of evil." You shouldn't have to ask for "insight" on the meaning of this command.

God told Saul what to do. It was so clear that there wasn't a hint of shadow or haziness about it. No interpreter was needed. His commands to you are equally clear. God says, "Be ye holy; for I am holy" (1 Pet. 1:16b). "Abstain from fleshly lusts, which war against the soul" (1 Pet. 2:11b). How much clearer do you want it? I've seen people get saved in revival meetings who got the message with no religious training whatsoever! One couple who were saved were involved in heavy addiction to marijuana. They had always found it difficult to quit because the drug is so affordable and available.

This young man and young woman stood up and testified that after they got saved in this revival, they went home and flushed the marijuana down the toilet. It was clear to them. "God, want do you want us to do with this pot?" Without the help of a preacher, they knew He was saying, "You just came to Me. You are new creatures in Christ." The old nature was saying, "Roll a joint. Smoke it. Party hardy, boys." The new creature inside said, "It's a new day. Get rid of it," and they obeyed.

When God speaks, it is crystal clear. Another young lady came here with a bag of mutilated audio CDs. She explained that when she went home after the revival, the first thing she saw on her walls were slick, demonic four-color commercial posters. The new creature inside her instantly realized their sole purpose was to reach out and suck the heart out of our youth. She looked around her room and she went straight to her audio CD cabinet and opened it up. Her redeemed eyes saw a cabinet full of filth. She didn't have to consult a Bible dictionary or call the preacher. She now recognized evil when she saw it. She took those things out and started beating them to pieces with a hatchet! Now that is what I call abstaining from all appearance of evil! Get away from it! It is sad that Saul never learned this lesson.

God told Saul what to do, but Saul decided to do things his own way, and he earned the rebel's reward. Friend, you are going to get what you deserve. If this statement frightens you, good. God has a wonderful life and a joyful eternity waiting for you—but you have to obey Him to receive His gift. There is no room for compromise with God. The Bible says, "Trust in the Lord with all thine heart; and lean not unto thine own understanding. In all thy ways acknowledge Him, and He shall direct thy paths" (Prov. 3:5-6). The Lord has told you what to do. Don't be stubborn and rebellious.

Saul didn't "make a mistake" out of good motives. He disobeyed the clear command of the Lord. He became a rebel when he boldly ignored the direct command of God.

He destroyed all the worthless items and kept the good ones. Are you like that? After the Lord saved your soul years ago, did you find it too hard to break away from some of those nice things God told you to leave behind or destroy? When the Lord said, "Get rid of it all. Destroy it all. It is history. It is Egypt. You have crossed over, so it is over. Never go back," did you get yourself a little canoe and sneak back to Egypt for a visit to the old homestead?

Saul disobeyed the clear command of the Lord. How about you? Even though God has told you what to do, are you living in direct disobedience anyway? The Bible says Saul spared the wicked king of the Amalekites along with the best of the sheep and everything else that was "good." The command was "spare not," but he spared. Saul's natural instinct and judgment as a knowledgeable man was to spare the best. *This is ridiculous,* he thought. *That is a good cow. How can a cow be evil? I'll keep this one and utterly destroy the rest.* Saul allowed his own interests to overrule the direct word of God! This is why the Lord warns us not to lean on our own understanding in Proverbs 3:5.

When God speaks, you have to obey, no matter what your head tells you. A man came to our meeting one time who was having trouble with his marriage. He got saved and then came up to the altar for prayer two nights later. I saw him pull into the parking lot earlier that evening, driving a beautiful Corvette convertible. I didn't know what he was struggling about until the Lord told me to say something very "spiritual" to this man. Frankly, it didn't make much sense to my natural mind, but I have learned to live in obedience.

I looked at the guy and I knew he was expecting me to say something dramatic, such as, "Yea, I say unto you, thou art a prophet sent from God. You will be sent out and the multitudes will bow to you." God had other plans. I looked at this married man, the father of one child, and I said, "Brother, before we pray, I have one thing to say to you: Sell the Vette." He burst into tears right in front of me and fell on his face. Why? The Corvette was his last toy.

After I told this man what God told me to say, we got down on our knees and I told him, "When you are out in that car without your wife, you pull up at a red light next to a young blond-haired gal who is maybe half your age. She sees you in that shiny red convertible, and you look back at her. Suddenly you are not married anymore. You feel as free as a bird—and you have even hidden your wedding ring—so you grab that wheel and rev the engine. Brother, I'm telling you: Sell the Vette."

He said, "God has been dealing with me about that car because, when I am in that car, I am a different person." Listen, *all* of us become like different people when we rebel against God. I am not against Corvettes, but whenever self-interest is allowed a place in our service for the Lord, it will surely cost us a price that we cannot afford. Saul disobeyed the clear command of the Lord and it cost him his kingdom, his sanity, his family, and his life.

Saul's sin found him out. The Lord Himself told Samuel in advance that Saul had not performed His commandments. God is always talking to somebody, and we had better not forget it. One young lady came forward in a meeting who was as wicked as they come. She just stood there staring at me surrounded by about three or four hundred people who had been saved in that revival meeting. I'm not sure how she ended up at the altar, but when I asked this young woman what her name was, she said, "You're a man of God. *You* tell me." I looked at her and said, "Sis, let me tell you something. My name is Steve. What is your name? I don't know your name."

Finally this young lady told me her first name and I said, "I say unto you, the Lord sought you as a child when your father committed incest. He has seen the pain that you have harbored over the years. It is like a cancer growing inside you. It is a bitterness and a hatred that you have toward all men." She burst into tears and fell to the ground, then she began moaning and groaning. She came up to me about an hour later and said, "How did you know?"

I'm telling you, friend, God speaks to people. God spoke to Samuel and He speaks to His servants today. I was preaching along one night in this revival when the Holy Spirit suddenly stopped me right in the middle of the message! He literally interrupted me in midstream, right in the middle of a thought. It would take the Lord to stop me in the middle of a message, since I just don't do that. I had to obey, so I turned toward the people and said, "There is someone in here—if you don't get saved right now, it is going to be over. You have to get saved right now." Suddenly a man jumped up from the congregation and ran to the altar! He came up to me afterwards and said, "This is what I did, Steve. This is my first night in the revival. I did not know God, and I didn't know anything about what was going on here. But I was so lost that I said, 'God, if You are out there and You love me and care for me, then stop that preacher in the middle of his message and have him call me out.' "

Saul told Samuel, "I have performed the commandment of the Lord," but at the same time this king was talking, the prophet Samuel was listening to something else. Behind the king's smooth excuses and claims of obedience, the old prophet heard the bleating of sheep and the lowing of cattle. Saul was telling God's man, "I have done what you told me," but Samuel said, "That's funny. I hear something different, Saul." Your sin will tell on you. It will find you out. "I thought you destroyed all the Amalekites, Saul. I thought you destroyed all the cattle and sheep. Wait a minute, Saul. Your sins are speaking louder than your words."

If you who are reading these words are a thief, then the Lord hears the rattling of that silver in your bags of loot. If you are involved with pornography, then as you read this sentence, the Lord hears the turning of the pages of those magazines. He hears it and sees it. God sees everything and He will tell the prophet. He will tell the preacher what is going on in your life. Don't try to tell me that God is not watching. He sees and hears everything. You have been found out.

God told the first murderer, "What hast thou done? the voice of thy brother's blood crieth unto Me from the ground" (Gen. 4:10b). When Saul realized that God had uncovered his sin, it scared him half to death. He suddenly realized that the Lord had heard the cattle and sheep when He was "supposed to hear silence." God spoke through Samuel the prophet and told Saul, "You rebellious, obstinate, and wicked man. All I wanted you to do was obey Me. Obedience is better than sacrifice. I don't want those cattle. I don't want those sheep. I don't want all that junk you pilfered from the Amalekites. I want you, Saul. You traded your soul for a few head of cattle and some bleating sheep" (paraphrased from First Samuel 15:17-29).

Is this where you are right now? Is this what you have done? Are you saying, "I'm living for God. I'm not that bad," while your sin is echoing through the corridors of time in the ears and sight of God? In Acts 5 Ananias and Sapphira sold a piece of their land and presented a portion of the proceeds to God—and claimed they had given it all. Yet their guilty hearts were sounding in the heavens. The Lord heard their secret scheme to hold back some of their gift even while Ananias and Sapphira stood before Peter. Obedience is better than sacrifice. God doesn't want your money any more than He wanted money from Ananias and Sapphira. He wants your life and He demands total honesty.

The eyes and ears of the Lord are upon us just as surely as they were on Saul. He is watching. He is looking to see if we are going to be faithful to Him and His word. Every act of disobedience is a direct act of disobedience against God Himself. God takes sin *personally*. Don't you ever forget that. Your rebellion and sin will always find you out. Sin is a tattletale. You don't know how many young teenage girls I have prayed for who had discovered they were pregnant. Sin is a tattletale. It will tell on you.

My last and most important point is that the result of your sin and rebellion is your rejection by God. That is hell on earth. The Bible says rebellion "is as the sin of witchcraft, and stubbornness is as iniquity and idolatry" (1 Sam. 15:23a). That means God puts rebellion in the same category of evil as occultism, sorcery, wizardry, and conjuring up evil spirits. That means that if you don't repent of your rebellion, if you fail to obey God and get right with Him, then your wicked heart won't be cleansed. That means that according to the Bible, God sees you the same way He sees a black witch or a warlock. Your rebellion makes you the same as a sorcerer or a psychic channel. Anything that sets itself up in place of God is an idol. Friend, if there is *anything* between you and God, then it is an idol and you need to get your heart right, and now!

One of the saddest passages in the Bible is the verse where Samuel tells young King Saul, "Because you have rejected the word of the Lord, He has rejected you from being king" (see 1 Sam. 15:26). I don't want you to hear those same words on the saddest day of your life. Don't be fooled or seduced by the enemy or anyone else—disobedience and rebellion are wrong. God has told you what to do. You know what is right. The Bible says, "Therefore to him that knoweth to do good, and doeth it not, to him it is sin" (Jas. 4:17).

Even now, you may be telling yourself, "At least I'm not as bad as some people I know. I'm not a narcotics addict or an adulterer. I go to church once a week." Revelation 21:8 is a frightening Bible verse. It says, "But the fearful, and unbelieving, and the abominable, and murderers, and whoremongers, and sorcerers, and idolaters, and all liars, shall have their part in the lake which burneth with fire and brimstone: which is the second death." Did you notice the word *idolaters* in that hellfire list? Friend, if you have set anything up between you and God, whether it is a relationship, money, or your career, and if you are going after that more than you are going after God, then *you are an idolater*.

I hate to say it so clearly, but I have to be direct because one day the Lord will hold me responsible for what I tell you on this page. In fact, *both of us* will stand before God one day, and He will also ask you about the words on this page. I urge you to obey God, no matter what the cost. If there is any area of disobedience, stubbornness, or rebellion in your life, you need to fall on your knees right now and get right with God. It doesn't matter whether you have been a Christian for 50 years or have never met the Lord Jesus before. You have been told what God wants you to do. Reject that rebellion and stubbornness before God rejects you and gives you a rebel's reward.

End Note

1. *Merriam Webster's Collegiate Dictionary*, 10th ed., 974.

Chapter 6

The Silence of God

The true test of a man's soul is not when he's singing in the choir. The true test of a man's soul is not when he's preaching behind the pulpit. *The true test of a man's soul is when he's alone.* When you go into your bedroom at night and shut that door, the real you appears. That is who you are, not the public man everybody else sees.

I have an old Webster's Dictionary from the 1840's, the kind our forefathers used to have in school. Do you know what Noah Webster wrote about "conviction"? He said "to convict" means "to determine the truth of a charge against someone." The 1996 edition of Webster's Dictionary says the same thing, but it stops right there. Noah Webster went a little bit further. He also said "to convict" meant "to convict of sin. To prove or determine to be guilty as by the conscience." Then he quoted the Scriptures! "They who heard it being convinced by their own consciences went out one by one" (from John 8:9). When you are convicted, you have been "found guilty." In the old days in the United States, little Johnny stood up to define "convict" and he read the Scriptures.

If God is dealing with your heart, I can guarantee you have fallen under conviction. When God speaks up about something in your life, you know beyond a doubt that you are absolutely guilty—without one plea. Your heart is beating like a drum, and you know something is wrong. You know you are not right with God. Part of you—the religious part—may be irritated and disgusted with me over my "fixation" with sin and holiness in this book. Another part of you fell under *conviction*. You feel guilty because you are not where you should be with God.

You may be a "dyed in the wool" Pentecostal with a public commitment to righteous living and the holy life of separation. Everybody thinks your walk with God is okay, but deep down inside, you may know you have a heart full of filth! If that is happening to you right now, you need to thank God that you feel guilty. I'm sorry to say that I know some people who don't feel it anymore. They don't feel convicted over anything. They're hard and cold; they've separated themselves from God. My friend, thank God that you feel something right now—even if it is conviction.

What about the seasons in our lives where God seems to be silent? What do you know about "the silence of God"? Perhaps you are wondering, "Where is He? Where is God? Everybody says He exists. Where is He?" then I'm going to tell you what is going on in your life right now. The Psalmist described your situation thousands of years ago:

> *These things hast thou done, and I kept silence; thou thoughtest that I was altogether such an one as thyself: but I will reprove thee, and set them in order before thine eyes. Now consider this, ye that forget God, lest I tear you in pieces, and there be none to deliver. Whoso offereth praise glorifieth Me: and to him that ordereth his conversation aright will I shew the salvation of God* (Psalm 50:21-23).

You may be one of many people reading this book who are questioning the very existence of God. Perhaps you sense an apparent absence in your life and are beginning to wonder if He's really out there, since you don't feel Him. Have you felt His presence recently? Do you feel like you are in control of your own destiny, that you can see no sign of His hand in your affairs? Do you say to yourself and to anyone else who will listen, "If He's out there, He's being awfully quiet."

When God is silent, you may feel like a ship abandoned on a vast ocean to battle the raging waters. Perhaps you can remember a time in your life when you heard the voice of God and followed His commands. At one time you lived under His authority and listened to His instructions, but for some reason you have drifted away. Now you can't seem to decipher His voice. You are like a radio that can't tune in to a strong station—you are lost in static, picking up only faint bits and pieces of broken signals from distant stations here and there.

Perhaps you can relate to the Psalmist's words, "Because they have no changes, therefore they fear not God" (Ps. 55:19b). When nothing "major" is happening in our lives, we tend to no longer fear the Lord. With no catastrophes threatening our lives, we lose our fear—and supposedly our need—of God. This dangerous pattern welcomes even worse catastrophes.

Some people think they have God "figured out." I'm warning you that God may be quiet right now, but He has a plan. If you are a Christian, perhaps you are suffering from God's apparent disregard for your prayerful petitions? Have you felt that God was not listening at times? Be honest. Have you been asking God to meet a need and received absolutely no response? Perhaps you've heard the old adage, "His delays are not necessarily His denials." Remember, faithful friend, many times God delays His response in order to work out His perfect plan.

My friend, you are in the right place at the right time, doing the right thing. You are reading these words because God has called you. He is speaking to your heart. If you are experiencing God's silence, I want you to understand that Jesus is still with you. However, when God is not making noise in your life, there could be incredible dangers lurking nearby. Don't think the spirit realm is quiet or motionless just because God is not making noise. Let me tell you what His silence does not mean.

The silence of God does *not* mean that "everything is fine." Some of us are so arrogant that we nauseate God. According to the Book of Genesis, God was so disgusted with the pride of mankind that He regretted ever creating mankind and destroyed everyone on earth except for Noah and his family (see Gen. 6:12-13). Man's arrogant pride triggered the great flood, and God is still nauseated today when He sees you walk around in pride and arrogance.

America's teenagers act like they own the world. They'll cuss you out in a heartbeat and they're sure they've got it all figured out (and they're sure their parents are stupid because they don't). They hop in the car that their "stupid parents" bought them. They sleep in a bed, live in a house, and eat the food provided by these same "stupid parents." They are too pious, haughty, and stuck-up to realize that just because they don't feel the hand of God pressing down on them, that everything is fine. It's not. The day will come for every teenager when Mom and Dad aren't there to bail him out, to pay his bills, and to provide for his needs.

Don't think that just because God is silent, that He is "thinking like you." Remember the verse in Psalm 50: "Thou thoughtest that I was altogether such an one as thyself..." (Ps. 50:21b). Friend, God said, "For My thoughts are not your thoughts, neither are your ways My ways..." (Is. 55:8). God doesn't think like you. Just because He is silent doesn't mean He has conformed to your narrow way of thinking.

How do men think when it comes to spiritual things? For one thing, we are incredible actors. We are masters at hiding our sins from one another. We almost naturally think we have succeeded in hiding them from God too. No, you can't hide a thing from God! Your wife may not know about that adulterous affair, but God saw every part of it. Just because

Mommy and Daddy haven't found the porno magazines under the bed doesn't mean God hasn't—He has seen every single page. He knows all about it.

The people described in Psalm 50 are all wrapped up in ritualistic, religious exercises. They were cloaked in religious garb, acting out their parts. They would win an Oscar today...but God hasn't even seen the movie. My friend, God is not thinking like you. You may have hidden your secret sins from everyone around you, but you haven't hidden them from God. He does not think like you, and He is not interested in watching you perform your false acts of holiness. Others may marvel at your glamorous white costume and countless religious degrees, but God has never been interested in whitewashed coffins full of dead men's bones. Friend, you haven't hidden a thing from God.

You may have a long line of fans waiting to pat you on the back and offer words of adoration and praise. Thousands of sincere people can say, "Billy, you are such an example to me," but deep down inside, you know where you stand. The sons of men may call you holy, but what if the Son of God says you are a heathen? No matter how much you sing about Heaven, you will still go to hell if you don't get right with God.

Maybe no one else has told you the truth before now, but I will: Friend, you can be baptized in front of thousands of people and go to hell on the same night! Do you want to know why? Because God sees the heart. Thousands of people may clap at your entrance and praise your works, yet when the saints assemble in Heaven, everyone will ask, "Where is he? Where is she? Didn't we see them in the baptismal tank...?" God will simply say, "He never gave his heart to me. She was satisfied with the praises of men. They believed I was thinking like them, and conforming to their will. I wasn't even there."

Thou givest thy mouth to evil, and thy tongue frameth deceit. Thou sittest and speakest against thy brother; thou slanderest thine own mother's son (Psalm 50:19-20).

Wagging tongues will earn you the silence of God. I have been in Christian circles for a long time, and I have had to raise my hand with the others when it came to confessing that I had been guilty of slicing apart the Body of Christ. When we get in our little circle of friends who are just like us and are all living for God, we begin to think that God thinks just like our little circle. We all talk together about the same things. "What do you think about that, brother?" "Well, he's not of God. Just look at the way his wife dresses!" "My my, you know, you're right about that."

Friend, God isn't in your circle. He doesn't think like you do—especially when your tongue is out there flapping in the breeze. He left a long time ago. We find it too easy to get together with our friends and buddies to "critique" the move of God around the country. "Why, that stuff going on in Brownsville is the biggest bunch of hogwash I've ever seen in my life. How do you feel about all that 'falling down' business, Reverend Brother Dr. John?" Everyone in our group somehow assumes that we have just pulled God into our little circle because, naturally, He thinks like we think. Or does He? He isn't there, friend. God just doesn't think like we think.

We tend to be very lenient toward ourselves, especially when it comes to forgiving ourselves for our habitual sins. We blow it on Friday night, and on Sunday morning we hit our knees for a quick "Sorry. Forgive me. Gotta go" kind of prayer. The problem is that God looks on the heart. He knows your repentance is only skin deep. You're going to do it again the next night or weekend. God isn't into quick fixes like we are.

America is suffering from the plague of greasy grace, and we think God is as lenient as we are. We suffer because we wink at sin. We live in an extremely lenient society. "It's all right, brother." We turn on the TV and watch a man walk up to a married woman and ask her out on a date, and we just wink at it. Friend, that would have been an abomination a hundred years ago. Where else in the world can a cold-blooded murderer be put in a hospital because he pleaded insanity, only to walk out free as a bird three years later to stalk and kill again? We are so lenient that we wink at sin. God does not think like us. He is not winking. He is watching.

You may think God has been kind to you, but He has actually been "tolerating" you for a season. "He understands what I'm going through. I can't help it." Friend, God does not think like you. He is a righteous, holy Judge, not a compromiser. You have reason to fear. You may be confused by His silence, but don't fall for the lie of the devil that says everything is okay. Everything isn't okay!

I've heard it said hundreds of times, "God would never send anyone to hell." God doesn't think like we do, and people are starting to catch on. They are beginning to say, "W-w-wait a minute now. Maybe God *will* send someone to hell. This is the first time I've really heard the whole thing like this. I could burn for eternity!" It's in the Word. There is a hell. There is a Heaven. Everyone has a choice. If you don't choose, you still lose.

We say that God would never send a man to hell because we are lenient toward ourselves, and we think God thinks the same way. Every pastor who has had to preach funerals for unsaved people knows what I'm talking about. The family members always expect you to say something kind—and untrue. A parade of people stand up and say, "You know, there was never a man like George. George was such a good man. He took care of Nancy and the kids. There was never a better father." Everybody is saying, "Old George was a great guy," and there you are knowing that "good old George" is burning in hell at that moment! The whole time, the Holy Spirit wants you to tell the truth: "George was in my office a month ago and he said he did not want Jesus. He didn't want the Lord and he didn't want to change. He wanted to be good old George, so good old George has joined all the other 'good' people who rejected Christ—in hell."

Meanwhile, "good old George's" family is thinking that God thinks just like them. They should read God's Word to find out for themselves what God thinks. The truth could save their souls, but leniency could land them in the same place "good old George" went.

God may be silent, but *He is watching everything you do.* We love to hear about how every hair of our head is numbered, but we hate to hear someone read the passage in Revelation 20:11-15 that talks about how men will be judged for the works recorded or written in God's book.

Friend, what if God is silent because He is busy writing? Maybe He is too busy writing to chatter with you. The phrase, "He will set them in order before you eyes" (Ps. 50:21), is military terminology. It has to do with lining up a platoon of soldiers to march forward. God could be writing down your sins to march toward you on Judgment Day. I don't know about you, but I'd prefer that God put down His pencil and talk to me. I've had a taste of earthly judgment, and that experience made me genuinely fear the heavenly judgment of God! Before I knew the Lord, I was busted 13 times for drug activities, but one time I got hit with a "double-whammy." The police rounded up about a hundred narcotics dealers in my city, and I was one of them. The strange thing about drug dealing—and sin in general—is that once you start dealing drugs and achieve a measure of success, everything will seem to be just fine. At times, I was making more money than my father made. I would come home from school with a roll of bills. I had money to party and to buy things whenever I wanted them. I even bought my parents things. Of course they wondered what on earth was going on with me. "He's got a paper route, and he's making this kind of money? Honey, I think I'm going to distribute papers." The problem was that a judgment day was coming.

One day, everything was going fine. Then the next day, a squad of heavily armed police arrived at my home. They cuffed me and shackled my legs right in front of my parents. Then they showed me four warrants for my arrest for sales of illegal drugs. The day finally came when I had to stand in court in front of a judge while the prosecuting attorney walked up with a long sheet of paper. Then he started reading my life history. He read everything that I had been doing for the past year. He described every move I made, every place I went, every drug connection I made, what color of clothes I was wearing, and even what brand of tennis shoes I had on. That was when my heart started going thump, thump, thump. I thought, *Dear God, they were watching me!* I was caught red-handed. I was guilty, and there was no escape. Do you know what I and my buddies were thinking all that year? "We've snuffed them, man. The cops don't even know what we're up to!" Friend, God is watching you.

God's silence *does* mean that He is patient—even though He doesn't think like you. I thank God for His patience. Have you ever noticed that the father of the prodigal son *never ran after him?* Do you want to know why? It would have been a waste of time. That is also why God hasn't run after you, friend. If your son is a tyrant in the house, you probably need to just let him go. He is a prodigal, and until he's eaten pig food, you'll never be able to change his life. He has to eat with the dogs, share their diseases, and catch fleas before he'll come back home.

Just as the prodigal's father never ran after his son, so your heavenly Father has let you go, friend. He's patient. He is waiting on you to come back home, but His patience is wearing thin. His silence is a sign that He is long-suffering. Yes, God can endure the pain of your rejection far longer than most of us can endure such treatment, but Judgment

Day is coming. Jonathan Edwards preached a sermon entitled, "Sinners in the Hands of an Angry God," back in 1741. He said, "The bow of God's wrath is bent. And the arrow made ready on the string. And justice bends the arrow at your heart and strains the bow." Do you know what "justice" is? Righteousness. It is righteous indignation. Edwards said, "It's nothing but the mere patience and pleasure of God. It's His patience that stays that arrow."

God is waiting for you, friend, but His patience is wearing thin. He is silent at the moment, but I have to tell you that He is holding that bow. It is only the patience of God that keeps the arrow from flying like lightning straight into your heart. Pay attention to me: God ordained that I preach this message and put it in this book so He could keep a divine appointment with you this moment. God is speaking to your heart. Have you sensed His silence in recent days? Are you wondering, "Where is God?" He has been taking notes, friend. He has been watching every move you make. Now don't forget that God has already done something for you that is beyond comprehension! He has already sent His only Son, Jesus Christ, to pay the price for your forgiveness and freedom. He is totally right in this situation. Whatever He judges you with, whatever judgment He delivers, *you deserve it*! Even so, He is offering you His Son as a remedy for the situation you're in right now. That is a far better choice than "getting what you *deserve*."

God is pouring out His Spirit on all flesh right now. It is no accident that this message has touched your heart; God arranged to put this book in your hands. You are reading and considering these words by divine appointment of God. Now you have to respond.

If you are tired of God's silence, then you need to ask Jesus Christ to forgive you. He will forgive you and wash you clean with great joy. This story has a good ending, friend—if you will order your steps aright and come to Jesus. All of

Heaven will come down in your life, but you have to get right with God. You need to get on your face before God and say, "Jesus, that is me. I need Your forgiveness. I thought You were silent. I thought You were thinking like me, but You were not. I am a sinner who is far away from You. I have done wrong, Lord. Please forgive me and bring me close again."

God is taking notes, friend, but He will wipe that slate clean if you respond right now. I remember the night at Brownsville a man wearing a pastor's badge walked down to the altar and fell on his face. He was involved in adultery and he was tired of the silence of God. He fell down before God right there and repented in front of everybody. He didn't care what anybody thought. He wanted to get right with God. Another pastor had been away from the Lord for years, pastoring a major church, but had lost the touch of God on his life. He was living in secret sin, but one night he decided it didn't matter what anybody thought. He fell to his knees and got right with God because he couldn't live without hearing God's voice for one more day!

Don't get stuck in your pride. Don't say you want God to work in your life while trying to avoid repentance. Forget it, friend. God isn't offering a special on "cheap grace." Salvation cost Him everything; it cost the life of God's own Son. You had better dump your pride and fall to your knees right now if you have sin in your life! God has broken His silence because He loves you. He is saying, "Repent right now. Come to Me. I want to heal your land and forgive you. I want to wash you clean, but you have to come to Me today—today is the day of salvation, not tomorrow." The warrants for your arrest were issued by the righteous Judge long ago. There is also a pardon for you, but only after you confess, repent, and submit your life to Him.

If you need Christ to forgive you and wash you clean, then drop to your knees as quick as you can, right where you are. Don't wait. Don't hesitate. If you're not right with God, if you feel like you're without a family, if you have no place to go, then God wants to adopt you right now. He's pointing His finger at you and saying, "You! I want you in My family. But first you must be clean and holy."

The Bible says, "Whoso offereth praise glorifieth Me: and to him that ordereth his conversation aright will I shew the salvation of God" (Ps. 50:23). Are you ready to set your life in order and come home to God? The Lord is ready to forgive, deliver, and save you right now. Pray this prayer with me right now, right where you are:

Dear Jesus, thank You for speaking to my heart. Thank You for not leaving me alone. Thank You for bringing me home and for breaking Your silence. Thank You for speaking to me. I ask You to forgive me, to wash my sins away. I have sinned against You and I have hurt others. Forgive me, Lord. Cleanse my heart and make me new. From this moment on, be my Savior, my Lord, and my very best friend. I give myself to You. In Jesus' name. Amen.

Chapter 7

Summit of the Last Hill

It was the first time anyone had ever seen rain. At first the people were in awe as they watched the rain fall from the sky. Puddles began to form, and then low-lying areas quickly turned into ponds and lakes. The waters began to rise so high that many of the round-the-clock parties and orgies launched with the coming of the rain were interrupted. Most of the planned weddings were conducted anyway, despite the surprising rainstorms. After all, things weren't that bad. Only a few people noticed the water beginning to bubble up from the ground.

The rain caught everyone by surprise. Before long, the rising waters reached flood stage. All the houses situated in low-lying valleys were engulfed and swept away by the torrential waters. The bewildered valley dwellers grabbed their possessions and headed for higher ground. It was unlikely that any of them knew how to swim because deep bodies of water were unknown to them.

About that time, something began to happen that no one had ever seen before. The graves and the tombs began to give up their dead. As the ground loosened, as the waters gushed by, the soil-corroded corpses began rising to the top. If you don't believe that can happen, then I want you to talk to people from Mississippi, Minnesota, Illinois, Iowa, Kansas, Kentucky, Nebraska, North and South Dakota, and

Wisconsin. They'll tell you about the summer floods of 1993, when the mighty Mississippi River flooded its banks and rolled through churchyards and cities in state after state. They'll let you know how the coffin of their dead-and-gone uncle who had been buried for 16 years, came right out of the rain-saturated ground and floated downstream on the muddy, flood-swollen waters of the Mississippi River. They'll let you know how the coffin of the man who had been buried just the week before rose to the top of his watery gravesite and floated down the river to the next town. Some of the bodies were deposited 25 or 30 miles away from their burial plots. The people in the days of Noah saw this on a catastrophic scale.

The hills became crowded. The noise of reveling inspired by the ancient Mardi Gras spirit was no longer heard throughout the land. Fear and panic were on every face, although you could still hear the occasional cry of a greedy merchant trying to make a fast buck by taking advantage of the crisis. With the arrival of the rain, there was a sudden shortage of food, and stale bread was selling at inflated prices.

Terror began to grip even the strongest of hearts, and houses perched on hilltop sites were filled to capacity with friends and family. As the water continued to rise, unfamiliar faces were shooed away from the elevated properties like mosquitoes on a humid night. Then the moans and groans of the bereaved began to pierce the air. A little child had drowned. An elderly man had slipped into a ravine gushing with water. His body was snatched away instantly and consumed by the merciless deluge. The waters quickly became polluted with bloated human bodies and animal carcasses as they rose even higher. At first, people talked about those who died, but soon the numbers of the dead had risen so high that it was no longer news. People were perishing—but everybody had lost somebody.

By this time nobody was talking about business or the "who's who" on the social page. No one cared about economics, or the ten top keys to personal success. There were only two words on everybody's lips: "Noah" and his "ark."

For the last few minutes, you stepped back in time with me to the days of Noah, just before the Great Flood swept over the earth and changed the climate and geography of this planet. It did something else too. Those floodwaters killed every land-dwelling, air-breathing creature on this planet—except for Noah and his family, and the creatures he had stowed safely inside the ark.

This ancient event is recorded in chapters 6 and 7 of the Book of Genesis, as well as in the ancient writings of almost every major civilization in the history of the human race. Why? Because it happened exactly as the Bible says it happened, and every tribe and race of man is descended from one family of survivors—exactly as the Bible described it.

And God saw that the wickedness of man was great in the earth, and that every imagination of the thoughts of his heart was only evil continually. And it repented the Lord that He had made man on the earth, and it grieved Him at His heart. And the Lord said, I will destroy man whom I have created from the face of the earth.... But Noah found grace in the eyes of the Lord (Genesis 6:5-8).

And the Lord said unto Noah, Come thou and all thy house into the ark; for thee have I seen righteous before Me in this generation. Of every clean beast thou shalt take to thee by sevens, the male and his female: and of beasts that are not clean by two, the male and his female. Of fowls also of the air by sevens.... For yet seven days, and I will cause it to rain upon the earth forty days and forty nights; and every living substance that I have made will I destroy from off the face of the earth. And Noah did according to all that the Lord commanded him (Genesis 7:1-5).

In the six hundredth year of Noah's life, in the second month, the seventeenth day of the month, the same day were all the fountains of the great deep broken up, and the windows of heaven were opened. And the rain was upon the earth forty days and forty nights (Genesis 7:11-12).

...And the waters increased, and bare up the ark, and it was lift up above the earth. And the waters prevailed, and were increased greatly upon the earth; and the ark went upon the face of the waters. And the waters prevailed exceedingly upon the earth; and all the high hills, that were under the whole heaven, were covered (Genesis 7:17-19).

Mount Everest, the highest mountain on earth, is 29,029 feet high. If the floodwaters rose about 30 feet above Mount Everest, then they rose almost five and one-half miles high as the Lord covered the whole earth. Look closely at the verses that follow:

Fifteen cubits upward did the waters prevail; and the mountains were covered. And all flesh died that moved upon the earth...all in whose nostrils was the breath of life, of all that was in the dry land, died. ...and Noah only remained alive, and they that were with him in the ark. And the waters prevailed upon the earth an hundred and fifty days (Genesis 7:20-24).

My message comes from the white space in your Bible situated between verses 18 and 19 of this chapter. "And the waters prevailed, and were increased greatly upon the earth; and the ark went upon the face of the waters." (white space) "And the waters prevailed exceedingly upon the earth; and all the high hills, that were under the whole heaven, were covered."

You don't have to tell me about all the archaeological digs around the earth that have revealed a portion of sediment pregnant with fossilized remains of animals and plant life. I'm not surprised that more and more archaeologists are beginning to say, "There must have been some type of great deluge." I don't need archaeological or geological evidence to tell me that there was a flood. The Bible says it, and that settles it—whether you believe it or not.

Step back again to the last seven days before the floodwaters began to rise in the days of Noah. After all the partying and mocking; after all the curses and foul spitting toward Heaven; after all the foolishness and ridicule of Noah for his righteous lifestyle and his tenacious commitment to his odd construction project; it began to rain.

Some say the rain was God's tears. I remember hearing a children's album produced by Agapeland. It featured a song called "Noah's Rebel World" that says, "And the Lord was speaking. He then began to cry. He wept and wept for forty days. He wept for forty nights. And though it never rained before in all the earth's long years, now up the ark began to rise afloat upon God's tears."

When the water finally rose high enough to flood Noah's construction site and lap at the sides of the ark, hundreds of desperate souls could be seen around the base of that massive boat. I want you to picture this, friend, because I'm going to take you to the sermon that was preached on the summit of the last hill. What would the last man alive during the days of Noah say to you if he could speak to you in the next 60 minutes? I'm about to show you.

Hundreds of people were gathered around the boat, even before the water had risen to their knees. Then the water rose high enough to lift some of them off the ground, and suddenly desperate souls began pounding on the sides of the ark with bloody fists screaming, "I'm sorry, Noah. Let me in. It's me, Noah—it's Zechariah from the carpenter shop. I sold you the tools. Do you remember me, Noah? I know I mocked you, Noah, but it was all in good fun. I didn't mean anything by it, Noah. I know me and the boys ridiculed everything you did, but dear God, Noah, don't hold that against me now! It's me, Noah, your friend from the carpenter shop! Let me in. Listen here—you couldn't have built this thing without my help! I'm out here with my wife, Noah. She's eight months pregnant, Noah! Dear God, let us in this boat!"

The waters continued to rise and the ark began to rock. Thousands of bloated corpses were now floating on the boiling brown floodwaters. The stench of rotting flesh began to taint the air. Buzzards and other scavengers by the thousands could be seen picking the flesh off the dead, with no regard to who the bodies once belonged to...the young, the old, the weak, the helpless, the sick. I'm telling you, friend, this is what it was like. (We were never taught this in Sunday school, for some reason.)

It was the "survival of the fittest" in those dark days. I can imagine what happened when dry land became scarce. Life was incredibly unsacred, and personal survival became the chief god. People were willing to do anything to survive. As the hills filled up with desperate flesh, violent fights broke out, and the voracious spirit of murder marauded the land. People had to die. Like starving cannibals consumed with a killing lust, they died by the millions. It was now kill or get killed, and the land was running out.

About this time, a small makeshift boat comes floating by. It is already loaded beyond its capacity and the brown floodwaters are only six inches from the rim. It carries a desperate family that is frantically bailing out rainwater and at the same time smashing the groping hands of flood victims floundering in the water and trying to climb into the little boat. The victims in the water scream as fresh blood spills into the boat and runs down its sides into the floodwaters. Yet the family continues to bail and pound the bloody knuckles of the swimmers flocking in greater and greater numbers toward the small craft. In a matter of minutes, the boat and the family it contains disappear under a writhing sea of desperate people grasping for their last hope.

Come with me now to the summit of the last hill. Charles Spurgeon wrote of a picture he saw that depicted a desperate scene of the last survivors of the Great Flood. Spurgeon said this art piece by an unknown artist struck him with haunting reality. It was a picture of a man who had been climbing up to the top of the last mountain while the floodwaters continued to rise all around him. He carried his aged father on his back, and his wife was clinging to him with her arms clasped around his waist. He had one arm around her while he clung to an old tree with the other. One child clung to the mother's chest and she somehow clung to another. According to Spurgeon, the picture showed that one child was just about to let go and fall into the floodwaters. The woman was also about to drop off. Meanwhile, the father was clinging to a tree on the top of the last hill on earth. The branches of that tree were beginning to break under the strain, even as it was being torn up by the roots. Such a scene could easily have been true as the waters covered the earth.

This family had climbed up to the summit of the last hill. Now, with his last breath, this man is going to preach a sermon to you, friend, a sermon from the summit of the last hill. What is the point? Jesus said, "But as the days of Noe [Noah] were, so shall also the coming of the Son of man be" (Mt. 24:37). Maybe you don't believe there is any danger coming, but listen to what this man is about to say to you. He has already seen the world perish. His family is gone. His uncles and aunts, his brothers and sisters, are all dead and gone. In the distance, he sees the ark floating off and he is trapped at the top of the very last hill. It's over and he knows it. Within a matter of hours, his family will be dead. In this brief moment, he says to you:

"I want you to understand that things are not as they seem. God is not winking at your sin. Don't listen to your friends. Don't listen to your peers. Listen to the preacher."

Imagine this man clinging to that storm-torn tree as his arms begin to burn like fire from the strain of holding his family above the floodwaters. With his last breath, he warns you:

"There is a way that seemeth right unto a man, but the end thereof are the ways of death. Don't be deceived by the pleasures of this life. Don't fall into the snare of satan. He'll make you think everything's fine. Then he'll snuff out your life. Sin will destroy you. It will eat away at your mind and emotions driving you to the brink of insanity. Sin will satisfy you until it has its claws deep down in your soul. Its evil will grip you and rip you.

"Sin will take a hold of your hand, America. It will kiss you on the cheek and whisper empty promises into your lovestruck ear. It will woo you into its bedchamber and lull you to sleep. Then sin will stab you in the back. Sin will promise you everything and leave you with nothing.

"Listen to me, America. I'm the man on the summit of the last hill. Sin will love you for a season and curse you for eternity."

You may be living in sin thinking everything is going fine. Well, we used to have a farm in north Alabama where we had a bunch of pigs. Every now and then, we would get one ready for the slaughterhouse. Before a farmer kills a hog, he'll separate it and feed it hog corn. He'll give that hog the best slop from the kitchen and anything else the little porker wants. That hog probably looks over at the other pigs eating slop and thinks, "I'm some kind of hog. Why, they love me."

If satan is giving you everything your little heart desires, what do you think he's doing to you, friend? He's planning to slaughter you alive. He's fattening you up for the kill. Don't fall for it. Don't end up being the guest of honor at his banquet in hell. You need to repent tonight. Come to Jesus.

The sermon from the summit of the last hill contains another warning from the man clinging to the tree: "Remember, 'the way of a fool is right in his own eyes' " (Prov. 12:15a). He would look at you and bluntly warn you not to be a fool. He would tell you, "I am a fool. Look at me. I'm the one clinging to the last tree instead of riding high and dry on Noah's boat. I've ridiculed Noah so I'm not with him. I'm clinging to the last tree on the summit of the last hill. My life is being taken from me, and my wife and kids are dying. Sin will destroy you!"

"Don't be a fool!" he would say. "Things are not as they seem. Don't be deceived by sin's elusive character. Sin is like the light of a fire that attracts moths in the night. When they get too close the fire burns off their wings and they perish. In the same way, the attraction of sin can draw you in with its momentary pleasures, but it will eventually destroy you."

The man on the summit of the last hill issues a final warning with a voice grown raspy and weak: "There is coming a day when God will no longer deal kindly with you!" His mind had returned to times just a few months earlier when he was eating and drinking and giving his daughter in marriage. He had gardens in front and out back, and cattle and sheep in abundance. He had everything a man could possibly want, friend. Yes, he loved it all. He ate the fat of the land. When old Noah the preacher came around, he gave him a few heads of cabbage and sent him on his way. But the preacher could never get through to the man—he was as hard as rock. But on this final day, he is telling a different story: "There is coming a day when God will no longer deal kindly with you!"

He would say, "I remember when the preacher came by my house. He always wanted to pray for my family, but I always said, 'That's okay, preacher. You don't need to pray for our family. We're doing just fine.' " As his grip on the cracking branches of this last tree grows weaker on the summit of the last hill on earth, the man sputters, "God will not always contend with you. His Spirit will not always deal with you. The time will come when there will be no more opportunities to repent. Yes, there's coming a time, whether you believe it or not, when God will have His say. I'm preaching to you, friend, from the top of the last hill."

America has been lulled to sleep while her ship is about to plunge over the waterfall to certain destruction. We are all in our bunks sleeping and our ship is about to sink. Don't be one of those hanging on that last tree watching the ark of God float off without you! The man hanging on from the summit of the last hill would beg you, "Get in the ark while the doors are still open! Get in the ark, friend! You still have a chance!"

And the waters rose.

I wish I could bring that man back from the dead and have him stand before you tonight. You can't get away from the judgment. You might be the last one who's judged, but you can't get away from it. You can't get away from God, friend.

I don't believe God was happy when the floods came. He was grieved in His Spirit that He had created man, and that He had to watch His children die, but He chose to give them a free will. They chose destruction, and it grieved their Maker's heart. Right now, that same loving God is whispering to your heart, "Come to Me. Give your hearts to Me. Let My Son, Jesus, forgive you. He is the Lamb of God who died to take away all your sin."

Eighty-four percent of adult Americans believe that Jesus Christ is the Son of God, but most of them are going to hell. That is empty religion, friend. Do you *know* God? Are you prepared right now to stand before Him and face your final judgment? Repent. It will make all the difference in the world. Ask God to forgive you and wash your sins away. Plead for mercy.

A young man in Napoleon's army was found guilty of treason after he was caught betraying Napoleon. He was found guilty and was about to be sentenced to die by the hangman's noose when the man's mother bolted into the courtroom and fell before Napoleon. She said, "General Napoleon, have mercy on my son. Have mercy!" Napoleon said, "But your son is guilty of treason, madame." The desperate mother answered, "I know—that is why I am pleading for mercy!" When the guilty are forgiven, they have received mercy. May God have mercy on America. Forgive us, Lord Jesus!

You may feel like you have all the time in the world, but no one on this planet has that guarantee. If you feel God's Spirit speaking to you as you read these words, don't resist Him. If you want Jesus Christ to change your life, you have to make a move—and there is no better time than right now! The moment you obey God and answer His call, your chains will snap. I see it night after night, friend. I've watched the love and power of God instantly change multi-millionaires and paupers, prostitutes and Playboy bunnies. Jesus has forgiven and rescued exotic dancers, real estate agents, schoolteachers, lawyers, and Federal judges. He has saved politicians, restaurant owners, and athletes from local football, baseball, basketball, hockey, and soccer teams. Scores of pastors who had fallen away from God rediscovered their first love and salvaged their lives, marriages, and ministries by running to the mercy seat of God. Listen to the man clinging to the summit of the last hill—this could be your last opportunity. Seize the moment, repent, and be healed and saved!

God sees your heart. I've watched killers run to Jesus and publicly confess their crimes at these altars, while those in suicidal desperation have laid down their guns and drugs and surrendered all to the Lord. Make the wisest move you've ever made in your life. Come to Jesus. Return to your first love right now. Repent and start over in Jesus! You don't have to understand everything about the cross or the Bible—all you have to do is believe on the name of the Lord Jesus. I'm giving you the same opportunity somebody gave me. I was saved because somebody told me that Jesus could save my soul, and I cried out, "Jesus!" I don't care if you are a backslider, or if this is the first time you have ever been asked to come to Jesus, I want you to pray out loud with me right now:

Dear Jesus, thank You for speaking to me. Thank You for not leaving me alone. Jesus, I have sinned against You, and I've hurt others. Forgive me. I repent of my sins. Wash me clean. Wash my sins away and make me new. Be my Savior, my Lord, and my very best friend. From this moment on, I am Yours and You are mine. I give You my life. Come live Your life through me. In Your precious name I pray. Amen.

Chapter 8

"Will Work for Food"

Before I met Jesus, I used to be a professional bum who traveled around the country panhandling. I had some consuming addictions to feed, so I'd stick a pillow under a girl's shirt to make her look pregnant and we would walk into churches looking like we were destitute. I'd tell a story about how my "wife" was getting ready to have a baby, and how we didn't have any clothes. We could cry on cue. We would do whatever we had to do to get pastors to give us money. "Do you think $150 would help?" they'd ask. "Yes, it will get us down the road." We'd go down the road all right—to the next church where we'd get another $100 in cash. Some of them even gave us restaurant coupons to eat in fancy restaurants.

I know what it is like to be a bum. I used to be a regular at Rescue Missions. I'll never forget the time I was at the Salvation Army in Colorado. All of us sitting there were starving—we just wanted to eat. But we knew the preacher just had to preach, and his rules were clear: Nobody got to eat until the preacher finished his message. He was preaching up a storm and screaming at us. Meanwhile, I could care less. I was hungry. I was sitting in the back when he started giving the altar call. When nobody got saved, he just kept giving the altar call. The guys in front of me were whispering, "Jack, you get saved this time. I got saved last time!" They knew if nobody got saved, then no one would get to eat. I've seen it all, and I thank God for saving me from it all!

There are folks in almost every city standing on the side of the road with signs that say, "Will work for food." God bless your heart if you've had to do this. I know there are some sincere people out there in difficult times, but a lot of them are bums who *don't* want to work for food. I love them all, but I used to do stuff like that. There was a panhandler's network out there. Whenever I met other bums on the highways they would tell me where to find the hot spots in the next town. "Hey, you can get cash at the So-and-So Social Services in Pensacola, and these people are wimps over in Averageville; they'll give you all the money you want."

One of my Christian friends went up to one of those people standing on the side of the road. He said, "So you will work for food, huh?" The man said, "Yes. I'll work." My friend said, "Here, I want to give you a Bible. Now I want you to read that book for an hour and I'll give you five dollars—that's more than minimum wage." Do you know what the man did? He said, "No, I'm not going to read that Bible for an hour." My friend was surprised. He said, "But I'm going to give you five dollars to read the Bible." The man again told him, "I'm not going to read that Bible. I can make more getting handouts from other people while standing on the side of the road."

I have a message burning in my heart that the Lord wants me to preach. You have to deal with anything that stops the flow of God in your life. Listen to me. I know what it is to have something stop the flow of God in my life. I was an alcoholic and a drug addict for years—a heroin mainliner who stuck needles in my arms. I've been addicted to a lot of things, but one addiction dominated and overpowered me more than all the physical addictions I've had in my life. That was my addiction to criticism—my criticism of others.

If you have the same problem, then I have to tell you in love: Deal with that critical spirit. Say, "God, get this beam out of my eyes. I can't even see." The youth director of the Assemblies of God of South Carolina came up to me the other day. He worked there for years as the leader of the youth, and today he is pastoring a church. He came up to me for prayer, and the power of God hit him twice in the meeting. He got up and said, "Steve, I am going after the anointing. I am sick and tired of the criticism. I get around people who have nothing happening in their churches. They are not growing, but they criticize everything that is going on anywhere the Spirit is moving."

Listen, do yourself a favor. Get good and sick of criticism and the critical spirit behind it. Make up your mind that you are going to go after God. Just shake loose and shake it off right now. I want God to move mightily in your life and church. I remember the time a good Southern Baptist deacon from a 6,000-member church came up to me in the parking lot. It must have been a hundred degrees that Sunday afternoon. He said, "Steve, I want you to pray for me. I want what is going on in this place [Brownsville Assembly of God]." I remember taking his hand as I looked around. We were out on pavement that was so hot you could have fried an egg on it.

We were all dressed up for Sunday morning service, but it didn't make any difference. That godly deacon went straight down to the pavement under the power of God! I looked at that Southern Baptist deacon laid out on the hot pavement and thought, "Dear God, that is an attitude we need to have. Lord, touch me. Touch my life too. I am sick and tired of this lukewarmness. I want to be touched. I want the fire. I want the power. I want it all now."

I have been delivered of that critical spirit that used to plague me, but God still has to deal with me about criticism from time to time. When somebody criticizes someone, I won't jump in anymore. I've learned that criticism really damages the Body of Christ and grieves the Holy Spirit. An associate of D.L. Moody named Ira Sankey once said, "It doesn't take half a man to criticize." It doesn't. Listen, pastor, if you have to tear down somebody to lift yourself up, then you might as well go build cabinets somewhere. You don't need to be in the ministry.

You see, hunger is the hallmark of every move of God—not men or programs. A dear pastor friend of mine from Canada drove through a winter blizzard with his deacon board and their wives. They were so hungry for more of God that they didn't leave our Friday night service until 2:00 in the morning. The power of God just overwhelmed them. I watched that man carry his deacons out of the church building one at a time. He was like a mule. He just carried those men over his shoulder, put them in their cars, and chose "designated drivers" who were less overcome by the Spirit than the others! My friend, if you've never had that happen to you, then you need to get hungry. You need to say, "I want more. I want God's power to come over me."

The apostle Paul told the Thessalonians, "For even when we were with you, this we commanded you, that if any would not work, neither should he eat" (2 Thess. 3:10). North America is suffering from a spiritual disease. That disease has produced widespread famine, uncontrolled crime, rampant alcohol and drug abuse, a breakdown of the family institution, and an increase in Eastern religions and cult activities.

To put it in simple terms, this nation, which once was engulfed by good, is now being bombarded by bad. We are at a place of total destitution. It is time for us to hear again a voice crying in the wilderness. Something must be done. "But Brother Steve, there is revival in the land. God has answered our prayers!" That statement scares me. Do you want to know why? It is too clear-cut. It makes revival sound so

"Americanized." When we talk about revival and say, "God has answered our prayers," we make it sound like a one-time event. It sounds like a popular "fast food" formula for revival: "We prayed, God answered, and poof! Revival."

Be careful. The people at Brownsville Assembly of God prayed for two-and-a-half years for revival before it came. Throughout every revival service, there are between 25 to 50 people praying for the people in the main service, with many others praying for one or two hours before each meeting. We don't take revival for granted. On Tuesday nights, as many as a thousand people (or more) meet in the main auditorium to pray for God to send revival. "But revival is already here!" No, my friend. We haven't seen anything yet. Revival in America has barely begun. Our spiritual land was once known for its abundant crops of love, joy, and peace. We sent missionaries around the world with the gospel. Now our nation is producing poisonous plants of hate, depression, and confusion. We have allowed ourselves to become overgrown with tares. Towering weeds have invaded our spiritual flower garden, choking out the sunlight that brings growth and beauty.

Rodents, bugs, and destructive animals roam freely throughout our spiritual landscape, consuming the tender shoots as they pop out of the ground. We need a move of God. We need more of the Lord. "But Brother Steve, you've been here since the beginning of this revival. How can you be talking like this?" I know what I'm talking about.

Just outside the walls of Brownsville Assembly of God—and just outside the walls of your church building or meeting facility—there are thousands who are going to hell. We've seen some people saved out of the neighborhood and I rejoice over those souls, but I can't get away from the knowledge that for every one of the youth and adults saved, there are a thousand more who need to come to the Lord. Now you know why I will always say, *"There is more!"*

North Americans are suffering like a bunch of bad farmers or field hands who have failed to tend the crops, and are now reaping the results. We in the church have also failed to watch over our land, our field of the world. Now we are all, sinner and saint alike, reaping the miserable consequences. Like a discouraged farmer at harvesttime fretting over a bushel of worm-infested apples or cussing over a crate of inedible corn, we peer out in frustration at our overgrown weeds, stunted spiritual fruit, and bug-eaten vegetable gardens in total disbelief. Our nation is in pitiful shape, but how did things get so bad? We think, *Look at all the work we did! We don't deserve these kinds of results.* Hogwash. What work? What spiritual labor? What effort have we put forth? What energy?

Who has labored out in the field of souls chasing the demons and devils out of the lives of our youth and children? Who was out there last night crying out in the darkness for the lost? Who is going to be up tomorrow morning at 1:00 or 2:00 in the morning praying for all the runaways hitchhiking America's roads on the brink of danger? Who is still crying out for this nation? People like this are few and far between. Who paid the price for a mighty spiritual harvest? "Wait a minute! I've paid the price. I go to church. I pay my tithes. I've signed up as a youth sponsor. I help take our youth to ski retreats and I'm involved in planning the big march in Washington, D.C. I'm going to let my voice be heard." That's wonderful. I'm happy for you. But did you know you can march on Washington every day of every year in your prayers? *There is more.*

Let me talk about the disease that is plaguing America (and maybe even you). The cure has been found; the vaccine has been discovered. But first you must admit you have this disease. Face it like a man or woman and get the victory over it. The disease is called *laziness*. It is a crippling disease. If you don't work, you don't eat. We want to eat the fruit of the

Spirit and feast on the things of God, but we don't want to do anything for it. The Holy Spirit woke me up early one morning and gave me this message exactly as I am giving it to you. Do you want God to come down in your life? Do you want miracles? Do you want your life to be changed? Let me ask you something: Are you willing to work for it, or are you looking for a free ride? Are you like most American Christians who say they want God, but expect their hired holy men to serve them God on a silver platter?

Too many Christians want everything laid before them. If you come into a church service, walk down to these altars, and say, "God, touch me. I'm waiting. You've got ten minutes...," You're wasting your time. Paul would be just as blunt to us as he was to the Thessalonians: "If you don't work, you don't eat." If you don't go after God, then you aren't going to get a nickel from Him. If you don't work, you don't eat.

It is ingrained in a man to work. If you are a man and you are out of work, then you probably feel like the most miserable person on the face of this earth. Most women do not go into depression just because they are out of work, but men will feel worthless. "Give me a shovel, give me a hammer, give me something to do! I can't stand this." Why? You were born to work, sir. It is the same way in the spiritual realm for all of us. We were born into God's Kingdom to *work*. We must work and go after the things of God. This is not the time for us to sit around pondering how bad things are in the world or in our lives. It is time to do something about it. Everybody wants something from God, but few want to pay the price.

People constantly ask me why great revivals spring up in other parts of the world but seem to bypass the United States. My answer doesn't make them very happy. I lived in Argentina where a mighty revival swept that country and brought great miracles, signs, and wonders. That revival is still going on today, but people rarely see what takes place behind the scenes before the evangelist ever gets up to preach. I saw a parade of tens of thousands of people stream forward to get saved night after night, but underneath the platform there were 75 to 100 people praying continuously for seven hours at a stretch. Those prayer warriors bombarded Heaven from underneath the platform, praying that God's will would be done. Those people were opening the heavens and binding demons and devils. *They were working for their food.*

That is what no one understands about the great revivals in South America and South Korea. Very few people understand the role that heartbreaking intercessory prayer has played in the revival that has descended on Pensacola, Florida. There are saints in each of these places who daily "work for their food."

If you want God to work in your life, then you have to deal with the spiritual disease called laziness. People tell me all the time, "I can't believe your energy." I tell them, "Jesus died for me. He went to the cross for me. All He's asking me to do is preach the Word. Any response or excuse other than, 'Yes Lord' is laziness, sheer laziness."

If you want God to work in your life, the very first thing you have to do is "get out of bed." Get up! If you are away from God, get out of bed. You are wasting away in spiritual slumber. You are fast asleep and the Bridegroom is calling. Get out of bed! God's alarm clock—that's me—just went off. Sorry, I don't have any snooze button—I have an order from God to wake you up! The only way to turn me off is to *get up!* The Bible says:

> *Yet a little sleep, a little slumber, a little folding of the hands to sleep: so shall thy poverty come as one that travelleth; and thy want as an armed man* (Proverbs 24:33-34).

The Bible says if you don't work, you don't eat. Are you lazy? Don't get mad; just answer the question honestly. If you are fast asleep in bed when you should be up and at work on some spiritual task, then you know why you are in poverty and spiritual bankruptcy. Listen, the sun rose a long time ago. It's time to get up! God didn't save you so you could become a lazy spiritual bum. God really wants to do something in your life, but you will have to "get out of bed."

Do you jump to attention when the alarm rings for physical labor and making money? How about the spiritual? Do you snap to attention or push the "snooze button" when it comes to spiritual labor? Charles Spurgeon said, "As to serving the Lord with cold hearts and drowsy souls, there has been too much of it and it causes Christianity to wither. Men ride stallions when they hunt for gain and snails when they are on the road to heaven." He had very little patience with people who labor for things that perish but sleep through every opportunity to gain those things that will never pass away. *Get out of bed.*

Every miracle in the Bible was received by action. Don't wait for Jesus to arrive in your bedroom while you lie there. Be like the woman with the issue of blood in Matthew chapter 9. When she heard that the Lord was coming, she staggered up from her bed of affliction and went after Jesus, even though He was in the middle of a swirling crowd of people. She would not be denied. You've got to get out of bed.

The second thing you must do if you want God to touch you today is to "get out of your house." By now you are thinking, *What are you talking about, preacher?* Your house is your place of spiritual security. You have built walls around you to insulate yourself from others. There is a good chance that one or all of the walls in your house are made from bitterness that dates back to the time years ago when someone in the church hurt you.

Years ago, a dear woman who was a millionaire decided to donate a $19 iron to the church fellowship hall. (This was the kind of iron you use to press clothes.) She made sure everyone knew about that $19 iron too. One day she went into the fellowship hall and noticed that the iron was gone, so she asked a member of the church where it was. This person said, "Well, I saw the pastor take it home. He needed an iron because his was broken." She promptly left the church!

When I met her years later, I was expecting to hear her tell me she'd fallen into an adulterous affair, had run into a major problem, or was dealing with a deep-seated bitterness or hatred toward someone. As she poured her heart out to me, I was waiting for a climax in her heartbroken confession. Then she said, "I walked into the church and the iron was gone. The iron *that I bought for the church* was gone, so I haven't been back since. I'll never go back to that church. How could the pastor take that iron that I had given to the church and use it at home?"

Listen, friend, if you want God to touch you, then get out of bed and get out of your house. That lady had allowed a bitter spirit to suffocate her life with Christ! There can be walls of sin separating you from God, whether they are walls of bitterness or of unbelief. "Well, I was ready for God to touch me at the revival meeting until I saw that Brother Wayne character fall under the power over there. I've never seen anything like that before, and my pastor said it can't be from God." If it is time for God to touch you, then it is time for you to see things you've never seen before. That is what made the early Church grow so quickly—they saw and experienced things they had never seen before!

Peter saw a sheet filled with unclean animals fall from Heaven. Have you seen a sheet fall from Heaven? The early church ran with the vision of God. The disciples ran with the miraculous as they followed the Holy Ghost. They didn't say, "Now wait just a minute, Peter! What is this 'healing shadow' business?" Yet the Bible clearly implies that people were being placed in front of Peter because his shadow was actually healing the sick! (See Acts 5:15.) Show me that one in your denominational doctrine book! Even Jesus didn't do that. Yet they were doing it after Pentecost—it's in the Word.

Is the "ceiling of your room" plastered with prayers of greed and selfish desires that never made it past the sheet rock? If you want God to move in your life, then you need to get out of bed and get out of your house of safety! Don't try to whip God out of your back pocket every time you are in a fix. Jesus wants your heart. He wants your life. You may be asking Him for deliverance from material bankruptcy when you need to be delivered from spiritual bankruptcy. "But seek ye first the kingdom of God, and His righteousness; and all these things shall be added unto you" (Mt. 6:33). God is not Santa Claus or a Spanish Papa Noel. He is not out there spending His time looking for little gifts to fill your dirty stocking with. God blesses people who go after Him. Don't get your priorities all twisted around. I don't believe we "earn a living" as Christians; we "receive" a living. The things we need are "added" to us when we seek first the Kingdom. Friend, every dollar you make is from Jesus. It's all from God. You receive a living because you seek first the Kingdom. Get out of that house.

If anybody "got up out of bed and out of his house," it was blind Bartimaeus in Mark 10:46. He was trapped in a house of darkness, both physically and spiritually. There was no hope. He was destitute, with no future. Then someone told him that Jesus could change his life. Somebody told him that Jesus could heal his blindness. He didn't hesitate. He got out of his house and he went after God. No matter who talked about him or told him to shut up, he just kept calling out at the top of his lungs, "Jesus, Son of David, have mercy on me! Jesus, Son of David, have mercy on me!"

Break out of that religious mold. If you don't work, you don't eat. I know you have "worked" because you are going to the trouble of reading this book and putting up with some very irritating statements from me. You must be hungry for more, my friend! You have stepped out because you want God to touch you. It is time to stand in the presence of the Lord so a shower from Heaven can come down. You are hungry enough that you have worked for a meal from God.

There are others who complain, "It is just so hard to live for God." If I was a general in an army and I had a private in my army who was like that, I'd kick him out in a heartbeat. "It is just so hard to serve in your army." The solution is simple. I'd tell him, "Get out of my army. I want commitment. When the bullets fly, you're going to be running. You could get me shot, private. I told you to cover me and you're out there hiding in some foxhole. 'It is just so hard.' Baloney!"

Guard yourself and live for God. If you want the blessings of God to come down, it won't be easy. My dear friend and mentor, Brother Leonard Ravenhill, at the age of 86, was still going after God. He prayed on his knees for hours and hours a day. I was with him just before he died two years ago. Do you know what Brother Leonard was doing the last years of his life? He was praying. He was still getting fresh words from the Lord because he knew what this Scripture meant: "If any would not work, neither should he eat" (2 Thess. 3:10b). If you don't go after God, you aren't going to get a thing.

You've gotten up. You got out of the house. Now it's time to *get to work*. God sees your sign by the side of the road that says, "Will work for food." He knows you are starving, that your life is in shambles, and your marriage is a wreck. Now He is telling you, "Get up, get out of your house, and get to work. Here are some tools; now get to work. Go after Me." Could you imagine if you were a boss and you had an employee who would clock in. He would go to his computer terminal and just sit there, motionless, like a zombie. This is how some of us are in the spirit realm. God has called us and we are sitting there like a zombie. God is walking by and He is saying, "Leroy, get to work; we have deadlines! Is there anything wrong? Do you have a life-threatening disease?" It is time to get to work.

Some of us like to play games with God, but He will have none of it. He is saying, "Get to work. It is time to get up, get out of your house, and get to work!" How do I do that? Pull up all those sinful weeds. Pull up that weed of pornography and the weed of rebellion. Pull up all those weeds of unforgiveness and bitterness. Repent and get all that junk out of your life. Get to work so you can eat! If you don't work, you're not going to eat of the fruit of the Lamb. Get your life right with God. Seek the Lord while He may be found. Pray this prayer with me right now, right where you are:

Jesus, I am sick and tired of being choked out by all these weeds. I'm coming to work in my spiritual garden. I want to see the beauty of the Lord in my garden. I want my life to change. I have sinned against you and I've hurt others. Please forgive me and wash my sins away. From this day forward, my life belongs to You. I am willing to work for the Bread of Life and the Wine of the Spirit. Thank You for loving me so much, Lord Jesus. In Your name I pray. Amen.

Chapter 9

The Romance of Satan

Listen, friend, satan is trying to romance you. I don't care how strong you are—he's a jilted lover and he never gives up. He can't stand to be brushed aside. You are being romanced by lucifer, the same one who tried to lure Jesus into his arms in Matthew chapter 4! A romance is a courtship or a love affair. It is an affair of the heart, an enchantment, a fling and a flirtation. It begins with keeping company and can lead to hanky-panky and intrigue. Ungodly fascination results in a deadly rendezvous. It is like playing with fire.

Lucifer wants your hand in marriage. Right now he's down at hell's jewelers picking out your promise ring. What do you want from him? A big diamond? No problem. White gold? No sweat. Rubies and emeralds? Much obliged. Intricate settings of gold wrapping around a full-sized carat stone? "Your wish is my command."

Satan is a diamond expert. He knows the color, the carat, the clarity, and the cut of the finest stones. He'll get you the best cut. "What do you want?" asks satan. "Your wish is my command." He's courting you. He's setting you up. He's standing outside the window of your heart serenading you with rapturous melodies of love with a heart consumed with lust. "I don't even believe in the devil," you say. Then you are in for a shock. The Bible not only says he exists, but it also describes him. It says he's a liar, he's subtle, and he's slander-ous, fierce, and deceitful. He is powerful, proud, and wicked to the core. He terrorizes, possesses, blinds, deceives, en-snares, and troubles. His primary occupation is to destroy all that is good, and he takes his work seriously; it is a very per-sonal vendetta. Peter said, "Be sober, be vigilant; because your adversary the devil, as a roaring lion, walketh about, seeking whom he may devour" (1 Pet. 5:8).

You have an enemy, friend, but he always masquerades as your lover. He's an angel of disguise, an angel of light. He is old and he is experienced. He has been at this from the be-ginning, friend. He started by deceiving other angels, and now he wants to deceive you. He has been at this for a long, long time. He was deceiving people when Jesus was alive and for centuries before that.

He is also very daring. He goes after big game. He even went after Jesus, Peter, and Paul. He knows where you're at. He is daring and he is angry because he knows his time is short. He is malicious, and if he is defeated at one scheme, he'll try another. He failed at Heaven; now he is trying to take over the earth. He is watchful and crafty like a fox. He's a wolf in sheep's clothing. John, James, and Paul wrote about satan and sin in their letters to the churches:

Little children, let no man deceive you: he that doeth righ-teousness is righteous, even as He is righteous. He that com-mitteth sin is of the devil; for the devil sinneth from the beginning. For this purpose the Son of God was manifested, that He might destroy the works of the devil (1 John 3:7-8):

Let no man say when he is tempted, I am tempted of God: for God cannot be tempted with evil, neither tempteth He any man: but every man is tempted, when he is drawn away of his own lust, and enticed. Then when lust hath conceived, it bringeth forth sin: and sin, when it is finished, bringeth forth death (James 1:13-15).

For such are false apostles, deceitful workers, transforming themselves into the apostles of Christ. And no marvel; for Satan himself is transformed into an angel of light (2 Corinthians 11:13-14).

If you consider yourself to be a theologian, and you intend to hyper-analyze this message, then you might as well put your pen down. God spoke to me long ago and said, "Steve, you are an evangelist. You were called to share My love and preach Christ crucified. Preach the simplicity of the cross and the dangers of sin." That is exactly what I'm going to do: talk about sin. It is probably going to sting a good bit. Early in the morning when I began preparing this message, I saw a vivid picture of a person sitting in the middle of a living room when someone knocked at the front door and at the back door at the same time. This person stood up and looked first toward the front and then toward the back. The tapping on both doors continued insistently, and the confusion on this person's face was clearly seen. He was obviously torn between the two. The steady tapping on the front door was at times overpowered by the heavy-handed banging at the back door.

I knew who was at the back door. It was someone bearing a gift that looked like a gift of love. It was wrapped in red foil and adorned with a beautiful, lacy-white bow. The gift bearer looked and acted like a friend, but I hoped the person answering the door would be careful. The giver's words were like the poison of a snake. His gift could blow up in the man's face!

Would you listen if your banker told you, "If you don't think out your investments thoroughly, you could lose everything"? Would you listen if a police officer told you, "If you continue breaking the law, you are going to wind up in jail"? If a financial adviser said, "If you keep living beyond your means by purchasing unneeded items on charge cards, if you take out loans for frivolous living and spend your hard-earned paycheck on unnecessary luxuries, you will soon hit rock bottom. I am warning you that bankruptcy is at the end of your spending spree," would you think twice about charging a large item on a credit card?

A farmer would tell anyone who was contemplating growing crops, "If you don't get up, climb into the combine, and sweep the fields while the harvest is ripe, you are going to lose the harvest. You will also lose your family's livelihood and all your income for the upcoming months. If you don't harvest the grain outside, you're not going to have any grain for bread inside. I'm warning you."

If you were a military officer, would you tell your troops, "If you don't keep your eyes on the enemy, if you don't pay attention to every possible form of attack, we could all be killed. I'm warning you"? Well, as a preacher of the gospel of the Lord Jesus Christ, I am warning *you*! If you decide to ignore the wooing of the Holy Ghost, if you don't take heed to this message, you could end up opening the wrong door! You might fall for a counterfeit and give your life to someone who is out to destroy your soul!

One of the devil's primary tools for evil is the deception of your own heart. He already has a great tool to work with because the Bible says, "The heart is deceitful above all things, and desperately wicked: who can know it?" (Jer. 17:9) You already have two strikes against you. Your heart seems to be ready to turn on you at any minute, and satan is dedicated to seeing that it does just that! Sadly, most human hearts follow the deceiver more than God most of the time.

Satan will see that his pleasures (sin) satisfy you until his claws have burrowed deep into your soul. He'll kiss you on the cheek and whisper empty promises into your lovestruck ear. He'll use his dazzling array of sinful pleasures to woo you into his bedchamber, lull you to sleep, and then use and abuse you and stab you in the back! He will promise you everything and leave you with nothing. His favorite lie is to promise you Heaven on earth and give you eternity in hell. He is more than willing to love you for a season so he can curse you for eternity.

Satan spares no expense in his courtship. If you show him ten cents worth of attention, he'll put on a show that you'll never forget (but wish you could). Perhaps you have already succumbed to the devil. You already feel like you are halfway to hell and can feel his claws around you. Your first step to freedom is to "realize that you've been had." Admit that you have been enticed and that you grabbed the bait. Don't worry about the excuses. It is understood that the devil came at you during the lowest point in your life. The deceiver likes to knock on your door when you are spiritually dry and worn out. The moment you flip on the tube, he is ready to lure you in. Begin by admitting your sin. I got saved *after* I realized that I was lost. Admit that satan has a grip on you. Don't be surprised if satan resists you at this point. Even while the Holy Ghost is working in your heart, the deceiver will begin to sing serenades and lullabies in your ear:

> Hush little sinner, don't you cry. Satan's going to bless you before you die.
> The world I'll lay before your feet. Don't be concerned for the Judgment seat.
> Hush little sinner, don't you cry. Satan's going to tell you the reason why.
> I'll give you fortune, wealth, and fame. From this point on, you won't be the same.
> My plans for you—there's so much to share. Trust in me. You won't have a care.
> If all these things can't satisfy, I'll give you more before you die.
> The preacher man says, "Turn today." My word to you is live to play.

There's so much time. Don't be concerned. You've come
   this far on what you've learned.
Your heart is pounding hard it seems. Don't turn to God;
   it's all a dream.
Rest in my arms. We'll sing a song. Together we will walk
   along.
This Jesus is a passing fad. They say He helps if you are
   sad.
The joy He brings is not like mine. I'll make you happy all
   the time.
So, hush little sinner. Don't you cry. Satan's going to bless
   you before you die.
The world I'll lay before your feet. Don't be concerned for
   the Judgment seat.

This is a clarion call to you, friend. You have been lulled
to sleep by the master of deceit. He is the king of backsliders.
Now it is time to take the second step to freedom: Determine in your heart to completely sever satan from your life!
Cut him off! He is romancing you. He's coming back for an
affair with you, pastor. He wants to have an affair with you,
church worker and Christian. It is time to cut him off! James
4:7 says, "Submit yourselves therefore to God. Resist the
devil, and he will flee from you." That means if you will do
this, he will do *that*. Let go of the hand of evil and take hold
of the hand of God.

I love to see repentance in this revival, but I don't like to
see people coming back with the same problem all the time.
They are "repenting," but they need to make some *decisions*
too. (By the way, godly, right decisions are a proof of true repentance.) Take hold of the hand of God. No man can serve
two masters. When you make a decision, it will keep you
through the hard times. It is like a marriage contract. No
matter what happens, I am married to my wife because we
signed a contract. She can go through bad times, but I'll be
there for her and vice versa. We made a decision.

It is time to break up with the devil, friend. Oh, he'll whine, "Well, can't we just be friends?" You tell him, "No, we can't just be friends!" Just count on that devil saying, "Can't we just do a few things together for old times' sake? You don't have to get so clean on me." I remember the day I got saved on October 28, 1975, at 11 o'clock in the morning. The devil had been beating me up for years, and he was shocked when I walked up to him and said, "I don't love you anymore! I belong to Jesus." Only minutes after I got saved, I went outside and started worshiping the Lord in my front yard. I had never gone to church and I didn't know anything about God. I was saying, "Sky, you are so blue. Trees, you're so green." I was born again, friend. Everything was so new. I looked like I was on drugs. But I had been born again.

Friend, I wasn't out there five minutes before a station wagon pulled up in front of my house carrying a bundle of a "dozen roses" from my old beau, satan. An entire rock band pulled up in front of my house in that car, and they were all friends of mine. Satan sent me the best gift he had when one of my best druggie friends stepped out of that car holding a big bag of pot. I knew the color well—it was Colombian Gold—some of the most potent marijuana you could get at the time. My friend held that pot right in front of me and said, "Come on, Steve. Let's go get stoned." It might as well have been the devil standing there saying, "Look what I have for you. I really love you. I'm sorry about those hard times. Come back to me! We'll make things right."

I didn't know anything about spiritual warfare, but I knew I had been changed. I looked my friend straight in the eyes and said, "I don't do that anymore." (I had only been saved for 30 minutes.) "I don't smoke dope anymore. I don't get high or run drugs." Now, I still looked like a truck had run over me because it takes God time to get the grave clothes cleaned off. I said, "If I smoke that with you, everything that is going on inside me will leave. A few minutes ago, Jesus Christ changed my life in my bedroom right over there. If I smoke that dope with you, it will all leave." He took the bag of pot and sort of crumbled it up, and then he got back in the car. One of the band members cussed me out as they drove off into the distance. Jesus helped me pass the test even though I had only known Him for just a few minutes! I'm telling you, your lying old lover will slink right back after you break up with him. Just resist the devil in Jesus' name every single time that deceiver shows up, and you will be fine.

Friend, break up with that liar! Tell him it's over and destroy any evidence of your relationship. Give him back every article of affection he's given you. Go through your closets in your home and office. Get rid of your whiskey and wine bottles, the porno magazines—burn everything he's given you. If it's something you can safely burn, set it on fire and watch the smoke go up. Break up with the devil!

What has the devil given you? You need to give him back his varsity jacket. Throw his promise ring right back in his face! "I don't want anything to do with you anymore, satan." Resist the devil. Snub him. Turn up your nose. Look him in the face and say, "You disgust me. I despise you, satan." You have to do that if you're going to get victory today. Tear up his love notes in all those worldy albums and CDs—they are from hell itself.

Once you have made the *decision* to break up with the devil, then it is time to open your eyes and heart to the *true* lover of your soul. Break loose from your wavering, unstable doublemindedness. Turn your back on the back door and walk straight over to the front door and open up to the Lord. Welcome in the true lover of your soul. He is not a taker; He's a giver. He's not a liar; He's the truth. He's not lost; He's the way. He's the giver of the best gift. He's not the destroyer of your life; He's the deliverer of your soul. He's not a roaring lion seeking whom he may devour; He's the

Lion of Judah seeking whom He wants to give power. He's not an angel of light; He's the light of the world.

I love Him. I don't know how anyone can live without Him, friend. To the architect, He's the chief cornerstone. To the banker, He's the hidden treasure. To the baker, He's the living bread. To the builder, He's the sure foundation. To the carpenter, He's the door. To the doctor, He's the great physician. To the educator, He is the great teacher. To the florist, He's the lily of the valley. To the juror, He's the faithful and true witness. To the jeweler, He's the pearl of great price. To the sinner, He is the Lamb of God who takes away the sin of the world. Hallelujah! Praise the Lord!

Now is the time for you to give your heart to the Lord—make your commitment for life and beyond. If you have already received Christ but have fallen away, pray this prayer afresh and make it stick. Do you feel like you live between two worlds? Do you have one hand in the hand of God, and the other in the hand of satan? Drop satan's claw and grab the strong hand of Jesus. Run into His arms and put your faith in the God-man who hung on the cross 2,000 years ago. If you want to live in His love forever, pray with me out loud right now, right where you are:

Dear Jesus, thank You for speaking to me. Thank You for being the lover of my soul. You are the One who bought me by shedding Your blood to pay the price for my sin. I belong to You. Jesus, please forgive me. I repent of my sins, and I ask You to wash them away. Cleanse me and make me new. Be my Savior and Lord, and my very best friend, dear Jesus. From this moment on, I am Yours one hundred percent and You are mine. I pray this in Your name, Lord Jesus. Amen.

Chapter 10

Summer Camp

The summer season is a time for many people in our society to kick back and relax. Students from coast to coast breathe a sigh of relief when the last day of exams finally ends—especially after the report card comes out and they discover to their surprise that they are advancing to the next grade. Summertime means water sports, family picnics and vacations, baseball, and iced tea. It is a time when the grass grows high right along with the temperature. It means more yard work for some, and more slumber time in the hammock for bums. For tens of thousands of teens and younger children, it means spending a couple weeks at summer camp.

Which summer camp did you go to? Don't jump off the page yet—everybody goes to summer camp, and there are only three camps to attend. You probably tried to write this chapter off as a "kid's chapter." I can almost guarantee you thought about bypassing this chapter in the book, thinking, *There probably isn't anything in **that** chapter for me. I stopped going to summer camps years ago.* I have a surprise for you—just stick with me for a moment.

I've preached a lot of messages during this revival. I've covered both the judgment of God and the mercy of God. I even walked through the auditorium carrying an ax one night. (For some reason, hardly anyone had any problem staying awake during that service!) All I did was tell the folks that if they didn't repent, God would cut them down. Now, I wasn't waving around some midget discount warehouse hand ax—I was carrying a hundred-year-old broadax with an ax head that was bigger than anyone's head in that place. I wanted to drive home God's urgent warning in Matthew 3:10 where John the Baptist said, "And now also the axe is laid unto the root of the trees: therefore every tree which bringeth not forth good fruit is hewn down, and cast into the fire."

A lot of people read that Scripture verse without feeling a twinge of concern until they learn that John the Baptist was talking to *religious people* when he said it! That is a hard message, friend. But, if you let God speak to you through the simplicity of this message, I guarantee that you will quickly find yourself registered in one of the three camps I am about to describe to you. God has one camp that He wants you to sign up for before time runs out. You may want to come running to it before we go much farther. I know two things beyond any doubt: First, this message is from the Lord; and second, it is no accident that you are reading this chapter right now. It is destined to either impact your life or the life of someone you know. Either way, I want you to stick with me through this.

My little boy, Ryan, went to a summer camp this year in the Midwest. He had the time of his life. Ryan was only eight years old at the time, and I was sure he was going to get homesick—when it would take a 700-mile commute for me just to reach him. I didn't know how to react when I asked him on the phone, "Ryan, do you miss me?" He just laughed and said, "What are you talking about, Dad? I've got a life—don't you understand? I'm eight!" Like I said, he had the time of his life and I had a major readjustment to deal with.

I know you've been to camp too. If you are convinced that you haven't been to camp this summer, then all I can say is you still have time to register. You have three camps to choose from. You may be reading this after a long day and you're tired. I promise I won't get too deep. You won't have to turn to your Greek or Hebrew lexicons. Just follow me as I describe the three summer camps you can choose from (just in case you still think you haven't already chosen one).

You might be settled into the first camp already! Some people have been there all their lives. The sign at the entrance says, "Camp Critical." This is the camp responsible for spewing out negativisms to all its little campers. There should be a second sign hung underneath the first one that says, "Welcome to the camp of the damned!" This is the camp full of mockers, squawkers, hypocrites, and blasphemers. You'll find the sign-up table showing up throughout the pages of Scripture. If you look closely at Peter's message to the crowd in Jerusalem on the Day of Pentecost in Acts chapter 2, and later in chapter 4, he had a group of lifetimers, some charter members of Camp Critical, mocking him just like they'd been trained to do in summer camp.

Look closely whenever you read about Jesus performing a miracle in the New Testament. Jesus commanded a man's withered hand to straighten out—and it did, right in front of everybody during a Sabbath worship service! You would think everyone who saw that miracle would say, "Wow! Did you see that miracle?" No, sir. Why not? There were some unhappy campers there. If you look closely, you'll see some card-carrying, T-shirt wearing campers from Camp Critical. They knew what to do. Things needed to be put in the proper negative perspective, so they stepped forward to set things straight: "Hey, what do You think You're doing? This is a holy day—don't You know You aren't supposed to be doing work on a holy day? What kind of rabbi are You? You can't heal somebody on our holy day! Why, that's nauseating—You just can't heal on the holy day!" (See Matthew 12:9-14.)

Some of us have attended Camp Critical summer after summer, and a select few have even gone so far as to sign up for a lifetime membership! They love Camp Critical so much that they intend to spend every single day of their lives in that rarefied atmosphere. They sat down at the devil's registration table with anticipation. Then they signed the dotted line and unknowingly laid down their very souls as payment for a charter membership in Camp Critical.

Camp Critical works miracles of its own kind. Its indoctrination fills you with suspicion. It is manned by thoroughly backslidden, lukewarm, and uncommitted counselors. Day after day, the activities and training teach you not to believe God, especially teaching you not to believe anyone who says *he* knows God (obviously that is impossible). You daily swim in the lake of lust, you dine at the table of demons during every meal, and you sleep in the bunk of blasphemers. What more could you ask for at summer camp? I can think of a few things! Listen, friend, if you are camping out at Camp Critical, haven't you heard enough? Come out of this camp of the damned right now!

The reason you're not saved or don't live in "victory" is because you blame this person or that person (just as you've been taught). You confidently point your finger and lay the blame on thick, "Well, *you* do this, and *you* do that (but I don't). He did this to me, and she did that!" You know the Camp Critical fight song by heart (it really isn't hard): "Gripe. Gripe. Gripe." (Repeat the stanza endlessly.)

You criticize everything. "I don't like that preacher. I don't like that church. I don't like the way he talks. I don't like the way that Steve Hill character shouts all the time. I don't like Lindell's hair. I don't like the music at Brownsville Assembly. I wish everybody would just sit still." (I can't list any more complaints—we don't have any more space.) The Camp Critical motto is: "Criticize everything." You criticize everything that moves. Every time somebody talks to you about Jesus, you skillfully turn the tables and dodge the bullet of conviction by counterattacking: "Well, are *you* really living for God?" Everything is critical and negative in your camping experience.

I'm warning you: It is dangerous when you receive counsel from crazed Christ-cursers or soak up the "advice" of satanic psychics. You have been listening to the critical comments of fellow Camp Critical campers, and now you are not fully convinced that God is visiting men anymore. You tell yourself there is no such thing as a personal encounter with Jesus. "Miracles are for yesteryear, and living for God in this wicked world is impossible." Friend, you might as well be a dope attending Camp No Hope!

I have to warn you that the day you signed your life away for a charter membership in Camp Critical, the fellow sitting behind the table was a spiritual blind man. He didn't know right from left, but he didn't let that stop him. When you hesitated before picking up the pen to sign up, he said, "Hey, just follow me. We're going to camp. I'm going to teach you how to walk and how to talk. I know where I'm going." The problem is that Jesus said, "Can the blind lead the blind? shall they not both fall into the ditch?" (Lk. 6:39b) Friend, if you are registered at the camp of the damned, you need to get out of Camp Critical as quick as you can!

You have already learned too much at Camp Critical. They told you, "We're going to teach you how to have a lack of interest in God's Word. We're going to warn you against secret prayer." Just so you would be a good backslider, they added, "We are also going to teach you to have a relaxed attitude toward conversion and revival this summer." You know you are backslidden if true revival truly bothers you. You know you are backslidden if your heart does not leap when a man shares how his life has been changed. You know you are backslidden if you are sitting there going, "Ho-hum, when will this be over?" while the angels of Heaven are doing backflips over the salvation of a lost soul, and Heaven is in a constant frenzy setting up more chairs for the marriage supper of the Lamb. Maybe God is looking at you and going, "Ho-hum."

The next day of Camp Critical classes features the core curriculum favorite: "How to Criticize Like the Devil." Every seasoned camper knows the routine. "I know you have a log in your eye, but bypass the log and look for the little toothpicks and little faults in other inferior people. Be like Brother Backslider and Harry Hardheart, campers. Let's keep that hard heart crusty, and look on the light side of the evil of sin. Sure sin is evil, but keep it light. It's not that bad. Don't get uptight, campers; it's okay every now and then to commit sin. God understands."

The second camp is the most dangerous of all the camps you could attend: "Camp Conviction." People all over the world walk around with conviction. They know they are not living right. Every time someone talks to them about Jesus, they fall under conviction—but they don't do anything about it. Millions of Americans have been indoctrinated in this camp of "the almost persuaded." Welcome to Camp Conviction, the American religion. Half of the people in this nation go to Camp Conviction every day. They know what they are doing is wrong, but they don't do anything about it.

Unlike the critical counselors at Camp Critical, the half-committed counselors at Camp Conviction are faithful to take you to a weekly religious rendezvous at church every Sunday. Why? Because they live in a state of conviction. They faithfully "pay their dues" to God like shopkeepers pay "protection money" to the mob. They know they are doing things wrong, so they figure they need to go to church and endure every service. Why? Because they are under conviction but don't do anything about it. It breaks my heart to see a pastor preach the Word of God with fire and authority, only to see the people just sit there with the conviction. He gives an altar call. He says, "Come to Jesus," but the backsliders are as cold as ice and the Christians sit out there nearly as frozen. No matter how fervently he pleads with them, they just sit there.

That is why I am asking God to bring back the power that hit Ananias and Sapphira in Acts 5:1-11. "Brother Steve, are you actually praying that God will begin killing people in church?" That's what I'm praying. That's what happened in the early Church, and you can philosophize about it all you want, but I think it was the greatest thing that happened to Peter and the disciples. At the very beginning of the early Church, people died for disrespecting God and fear spread throughout the land. You know what people said after that incident? "Don't mess with them. And don't you say you belong to them if you don't. Either you are in or you are out. People die when they lie in that church." Friend, I'm asking God to bring that back into our sanctuaries in America. We need to rediscover a healthy fear of God again.

You are a camper at Camp Conviction if you hang out around the cross every day, but you never get on it. You see, man-made religion is "hanging around the cross," but Christianity is "getting *on* the cross." There is a big difference. Every weekend, millions of Americans gather together to hang around the cross. They blindly sing powerful songs while ignoring their power, songs like, "Here We Are," "Just As I Am," and "Amazing Grace." I love church and I love those songs, but when nothing is going on in the inside, in the heart, then it is all an outward show. People just experience an emotional touch, but they never allow God to change their lives. That is Camp Conviction, and I'm sick of it.

King Agrippa attended this procrastination station. Do you remember what he told the apostle Paul? He said, "Almost thou persuadest me to be a Christian" (Acts 26:28b).

"Almost thou persuadest me to be a Christian" is the creed of Camp Conviction. That man was sitting there with the apostle Paul, the man who penned most of the New Testament books. "Here I am, Paul. I'm almost there, but I'm not all the way in—after all, I belong to Camp Conviction." Are you sitting on the same fence of indecision? How long are you going to stay in the camp where cutting counselors conduct classes on the many excuses you can use to justify why you don't have to run to the cross? How long will you allow those drill demons to fill your wishy-washy heart with excuses from the chambers of hell?

Every Camp Conviction counselor spends extra time preparing you for the moment you hear those dreaded words, "Won't you come to the Lord tonight?" Eagerly the counselors quiet their class and say, "Listen to this God-proof excuse: 'I am waiting until I understand more about Christianity.' After all, everybody knows you don't have to get saved until you understand more about Christianity, campers! Here's another one: 'I am waiting for the perfect time.' " Such is the camper's course at Camp Conviction.

I often preach on "the three conditions of the heart" during our revival services, and they correspond directly to the three summer camps of the spirit realm. The first condition is a "natural heart." It is naturally hard and cold because it is dead apart from God. The second condition of the heart is an "awakened heart"—this is Camp Conviction. The awakened heart has heard the truth *but has done nothing about it.* Unfortunately, no matter how "awake" you are, it will not save you.

You are in Camp Conviction if you feel the convicting power of the Holy Ghost and say, "I've never felt like this in my life," yet don't do anything but spout lines from your Camp Conviction "Excuse and Escape Book." "I am waiting until I have enjoyed the world enough." "I am waiting until I find a group of perfect Christians that I can be a part of." At

Camp Conviction, the most experienced counselors will tell you, "Wait until all your friends make a commitment." The reason Camp Conviction is such a dangerous place to be is because they will *let you fall under conviction* there! They don't mind if you listen to the Word of God and hear the truth. They will even let you be around gospel preaching. Why, your Camp Conviction counselors will even let you out of camp to attend the Brownsville Revival!

The only problem is that right around the "altar call time," the counselors will sit on your shoulders and say, "Boy, this was really good tonight, but it is time to go. You can deal with this back at camp, or even in your own home. Come on, we'll talk about this together over some pizza—you don't need to get radical and go down to the altar and give your life to Christ right now. Let's go before it's too late to order our food."

That's Camp Conviction. Don't fall for it. You'll be left hanging around the cross instead of getting on it. Campers from Camp Conviction always find themselves munching on bland meals of mediocrity prepared by lukewarm camp guides who will only take them far enough to get a good dose of conviction. You'll get just enough to wake you up, but never enough to go all the way to the cross. It is the camp of the awakened heart, but not the changed heart.

If you mean business with God, and you are still stuck in Camp Critical or Camp Conviction, then it is time for you to run for your life! As soon as the counselors turn off the lights, jump out of your bunk and race to the cross! Get out of those camps, friend. They are damning your soul. It is time to transfer your registration to the last and best camp of all: "Camp Conversion."

The motto of this camp is: "If any man be in this camp, 'he is a new creature: old things are passed away; behold, all things are become new.'" This is a camp of commitment, where the teachings of the Holy Ghost rule and reign. This is the camp of Calvary, the camp of the cross, the camp of Christ. I have to warn you that it is also known as the camp of change.

This is the camp where you can go in "down and out" and come out "up and in." This is the place where worn-out, sin-saturated, confused, bound up, tied down, shackled men, women, and children are transformed into Holy Ghost-filled, on fire, radical, blood-washed, sin-free, Spirit-led, devil-chasing sons and daughters of God! I just love this camp. "Yessiree, Camp Conversion is where I want to be!"

Summer has almost passed, but you still have time to go to camp. No matter where you came from, you can go to Camp Conversion and come away radically changed. When you go there, you are going to find some old-timers and regulars there too. You'll find Zacchaeus and his family, the jailer and his family, Elijah, Elisha, Jeremiah, Peter, Paul, and Mary. You are going to find George Whitefield, John and Charles Wesley, Jonathan Edwards, Charles Finney, and tens of thousands of blood-washed converts who came to Jesus Christ in this revival. They are all together at the cross at Camp Conversion!

> It's summertime, hip-hip-hooray! Now is the time to run and play.
> It's time to frolic with my friends. Go off to camp. There is no end.
> Camp Critical is the place to be, where everything is bad to me.
> Christ crucified is an age-old tale. Don't preach to me that message stale.
> I'm free as a bird at camp this year. No Holy Ghost makes me draw near.
> You waste your time with words of love, that God came down from His home above.

I've got friends across the way, in Camp Conviction they
   live today.

You smite their hearts with God's holy Word, but nothing
   changes is what I've heard.

They listen, they clap, they shed a tear, but at altar time
   they won't draw near.

"Put it off today, the Lord can wait." At Camp Conviction
   it's never too late.

But down the river, through the dale, there's a camp, my
   friend, I know of well.

It's a camp of change, a camp of grace, a place where conversions will take place.

The counselors all know the Son, they tell you how your
   life was won.

On Calvary, the rugged tree, He died for you, He died for
   me.

So think, my friend, where to attend, before this summer
   comes to an end.

Camp Conversion is the place to be. Enter in today, for
   eternity.

One of the things that I have discovered about Americans is that many of us aren't really who we say we are. We
are just a bunch of kids trying to find life and true happiness.
We have big adult-sized toys, but we are a bunch of children
who have lost our way. There is much more that can be said
about these three camps, but I know you understand how
important it is to escape from Camp Critical and Camp Conviction at all cost. If you know your heart is not right with
God, why don't you come the rest of the way to Calvary?
That is like driving 2,000 miles to attend a revival service and
failing to walk the last 25 feet to fall at the feet of Jesus!

This is your opportunity to straighten out everything that
is crooked in your life. Come to Jesus Christ and repent of
your sins right now. Ask Him to wash your sins away—He is
waiting to hear your voice. Move out of Camp Critical. Leave

the gates of Camp Conviction behind you and move into Camp Conversion—even if this is your very first encounter with God. If you are already a Christian but feel trapped in Camp Critical or Camp Conviction, then your deliverance is only a prayer away! My friend, pray this prayer with me right now, wherever you are at this moment. God is waiting:

> *Dear Jesus, thank You for loving me. I am sick and tired of my critical ways and half-hearted attempts to be like You. I am ready for a radical conversion into a new creation. Jesus, I have sinned against You, and I've hurt others. Forgive me. I repent of my sins. Make me new and empower me to live a victorious life in You. From this moment on, I am Yours and You are mine. I give You my life. Come live Your life through me. In Your precious name I pray. Amen.*

Chapter 11

The Arrows of the Lord

I was napping on the couch in my living room when I heard a hissing sound: *s-h-h-h*. When I opened my eyes, I saw three arrows fly through the air! Then I saw people stumbling toward me with arrows sticking out of their bodies and I realized they had been hit by *the arrows of the Lord*. Oddly enough, these people weren't sitting in the church; they had stumbled out of the church door and were headed for home. In this vision, I heard one man tell his wife and family repeatedly, "Man, I've been hit! Something is happening to me." (But he didn't change.)

"Now when they heard this, they were pricked in their heart, and said unto Peter and to the rest of the apostles, Men and brethren, what shall we do?" (Acts 2:37). Peter was preaching the gospel of Jesus Christ when these people were *pricked in their hearts*. God has a bow and arrow, and the Bible says, "Thine arrows are sharp…" (Ps. 45:5), and "His arrow shall go forth as the lightning" (Zech. 9:14b). David said, "For Thine arrows stick fast in me" (Ps. 38:2a).

The men and women listening to Peter's sermon were "pricked in their heart." That means they were pierced thoroughly, agitated violently, or stung "to the quick" (until it bleeds).[1] Many people respond to the piercing, stinging arrows of God by repenting of their sin and receiving Jesus Christ as their Lord and Savior. But some do not respond that way. "Then they that gladly received his word were baptized: and the same day there were added unto them about three thousand souls" (Acts 2:41).

Imagine a crowd gathered in your town with Baptists from Birmingham, Methodists from Miami, Pentecostals from Paducah, atheists from Atlanta, Mormons from Mississippi, Catholics from California, drug addicts from Wall Street, sick people from Sacramento, ex-cons, pastors, Sunday school teachers, lawyers, doctors, bums, vacuum cleaner salesmen, honor roll students, media moguls, newspaper boys, butchers, bakers, and candlestick makers. What if they were all in the right place at the right time under divine appointment?

Think about the devout Jews standing in that Jerusalem street. They came from all walks of life and represented the key language groups of the known world. They marveled when they heard the gospel preached so powerfully by an unlearned fisherman and reinforced by people who were speaking in so many different tongues. God speaks *your* language too—no matter what you speak or what culture you identify with. You can be a drug addict from the 'hood or a banker from Georgia, but He will speak your language perfectly. God even knows how to speak to Mary Kay Cosmetics consultants, public school teachers, doctors, street workers, prostitutes, businessmen, students, and homeless kids in Mexico City's dumps!

Suppose one of the people in that crowd was David, an 18-year-old Jewish boy standing with his older brother, Samuel. The older brother continually talked negatively about this Jesus called "Messiah" (Christ). Both of them had been at the Lord's crucifixion, but David had slipped away from Samuel. (If you are hanging around negative people and you want to get your heart right with God, you have to slip away.) Crowds of people had come to watch Jesus die on the hill of the skull, and they sat down in small groups to watch the three condemned men die, just like we sit down to watch a movie. I believe the literal blood of Jesus attracted people. People love blood and gore, so they always came to watch crucifixions, but the fame of this man generated even more interest.

David didn't want to watch this event from a "safe distance" like Samuel, who just wanted to "check out" this rabbi who said He was the Son of God. David worked his way right up to the foot of the cross in the growing darkness. First he looked toward the base of the cross and saw Roman soldiers gambling for the man's garment in total disregard for His suffering. Their indifference disgusted the 18-year-old boy, who thought, *That man above their heads is dying while they cuss and fuss over His garment like schoolboys.* David looked closely at the soil nearest the foot of the cross. It was soaked with blood. Drops of blood were splattered on the ground further away from the cross too, having fallen to the ground from the man's bleeding head and suspended arms.

David focused his eyes on the feet of Jesus in the dim light and saw the massive hand-hewn iron nail piercing His bruised flesh. Blood was still pouring from the enlarged wounds torn when the cross was dropped roughly into the ground. The blood was running over His toes, creating a steady stream of crimson running down the Roman cross to the earth. David's eyes traced the stream of blood upward, and he saw the man's legs tremble under the sheer agony and physical shock of crucifixion. One glance at the Lord's midsection brought a bright red flush of embarrassment to David's face when he suddenly realized this man had been suspended helplessly in front of His tormentors while totally naked, fully exposed to His mockers and critics. He was dying in total humiliation. Then David noticed that many people in the crowd were mumbling and grumbling, or even laughing as they looked at the man on the cross and shouted, "If You are *really* the Son of God, then come off the cross! See, He saved others, but He can't even save Himself!

Look at Him up there. Hey, Jesus, come on down. Where are Your angels now? Hey, You! We saw You raise Lazarus from the dead. Can't You jerk Your hands off those nails?"

David was startled by the contrast between the man and His critics. Then David's eyes focused on the hands of the crucified man. They were rough and callused, the hands of a working man. But now they were covered in blood. They would never work again. As David stared at the Lord's hands, he glimpsed the man on the right and the man on the left. They were dying too, but they were dying differently.

Again he looked at the Lord Jesus and instantly perceived that the man in the middle was innocent. Right about that time he snapped to attention. David looked up at the Lord Jesus and quickly edged closer. He could just barely hear Him say, "Father, forgive them; for they know not what they do." These words pierced David's soul like an arrow and he buckled over in pain as if from a physical wound. He hurt so much deep down inside that he began to back away blindly and tripped over some onlookers. They looked at him in disgust and snapped, "Watch where you're going, stupid boy!" He turned around and tried to insult them in return, but instead he just mumbled, "I'm sorry."

He was too shaken by what he had seen at the cross to argue with anyone. He couldn't forget the pain of those words that kept ringing in his ears, "Father, forgive them; for they know not what they do." How can I be so certain these things took place at the cross? The Bible says that after the Lord was crucified, the people left "smiting their breasts" (see Lk. 23:48). In the Jewish culture, that meant they knew they were guilty, that something was terribly wrong. They had been struck by the arrows of the Lord that dark day.

Then the words that were meant for evil came back to David: "Watch where you're going, stupid boy!" He began to ask himself, "Where *am* I going? What is going on in my life, and what is happening to me? What would happen if I was dying on that cross? Where would I spend eternity?" David was experiencing what the Bible calls "conviction."

If you put up a billboard by the highway that says, "For God so loved the world, that He gave His only begotten Son," some of the people would curse you as a "stupid religious person" and say, "I wish those Christians would spend their money on something more worthwhile—like feeding the poor. I wish they would quit shoving Jesus in my face." A woman in the car right behind them might look up at the same message and say, "Dear God, You still love me. Jesus, I hope You understand where I'm going tonight. I hope You can help me!" Why? The same message that hardens one person can soften another.

The Holy Spirit used even the harsh words of hardened onlookers at the crucifixion to convict young David of his sin. "Watch where you're going, stupid boy!" The Spirit also caused David to remember the prayer of Jesus on the cross: "Father, forgive them; for they know not what they do." David was thinking about Jesus. *If He is dying, then who am I going to talk to? Does this man really know the heavenly Father?*

Many people in our secular society know nothing about God. I remember praying for a drug addict one night right in the revival—he was like a kid at "Toys R Us"! He was going berserk. He had never, ever experienced anything like this. You never know what's going on in a man's heart. He can have an ounce of pot hanging out his pocket with needles sticking out and be cussing up a storm while, at the same time, he is listening to this preacher and thinking, *That makes sense.* This is also true with gospel music. I know that unsaved people will play gospel tapes. Why? Because those tapes speak to them. Those songs answer nagging questions planted in their hearts by the Holy Spirit. You never know what is going on in a man's heart.

When the man, Jesus Christ, finally died, the sky was totally black even though it was midday in Jerusalem. The crowds were very uneasy about it all. David managed to find his brother, Samuel, who was still standing a considerable distance away from the cross. David was under heavy conviction of the Holy Ghost, but Samuel, who had maintained a comfortable distance from the cross, had kept his heart cold and distant. He greeted his younger brother and said, "See, David? There, I told you. Look at Him. He just hung His head. He's dead. Did you see the spear—that Roman soldier just pierced Him and He didn't move. He's dead. Like I told you, David, He wasn't the Son of God. Come on, let's get out of here."

It was only a few days later that the two brothers showed up in the crowd on the Day of Pentecost and heard Peter preach the gospel. Another pair was listening intently that day too. Elizabeth and her little daughter, Ruthie, also listened to Peter's inspired words. They had never heard anything like it, although they had seen Jesus heal a blind man with their own eyes a few months earlier. Little Ruthie had dropped a coin in the blind man's bucket just the day before, and when they walked through the marketplace the next day, they saw Jesus of Galilee heal the man's eyes right in front of everybody. They couldn't believe it when the man who had been blind suddenly jumped up and shouted, "I can see!" He ran all over the marketplace after he hugged the Teacher. Little Ruthie was so excited when she saw it that it was the main topic of conversation for days on end around the dinner table.

Little Ruthie was only eight and she had a question that just wouldn't wait. She sat down at the table, turned to Mommy and Daddy, and asked, "How could that man open the blind man's eyes if God is not with Him, Daddy?" Her daddy hung his head and said, "I don't understand it. But I was just talking to our neighbor, Jeremiah, who's a strong leader in the synagogue. He said it was some type of sorcery. I just don't know, Ruthie."

It was no accident that Ruthie and her mother, Elizabeth, found themselves near the front of the crowd listening to the preaching of Peter, surrounded by devout Jews from all over the world. What did they hear? They heard the zeal of an "on-fire, blood-washed, Heaven-sent, uncompromising, sold-out, known-in-hell, Holy Ghost preacher" named Peter!

God launched three arrows on that Day of Pentecost. The first arrow of God came against the claims that God's servants were drunk. Peter quoted from the Book of Joel and said the people from the upper room were not drunk, but were filled with the Holy Spirit. That is when God pulled back the string of His bow and shot His sharp arrow straight into the hearts of the people. Then He notched arrow number two, smoothly pulled back the bowstring to His cheek, and prepared to fire. The arrow was straight and the tip was incredibly sharp. Once fired, that arrow would fly with unworldly strength and enough velocity to go right through the bull's eye of human souls.

When Peter told the crowd that the disciples were there because of Jesus of Nazareth, the One whom God mightily used to perform wonders right in the crowd's midst, the second convicting arrow of God flew straight into their hearts. Elizabeth and Ruthie were standing directly in front of the bow of God, and as soon as Peter's words rang out, little Ruthie looked up at Elizabeth and said, "Mommy, he's talking about the miracle we saw the other day when that blind man opened his eyes!" Elizabeth turned to Ruthie in tears and said, "I think you're right, honey. I think that man Jesus was more than just a miracle-worker. He is not what Daddy said He was. He wasn't a sorcerer. This man Peter knows who He was."

Peter glanced at the teenaged David and said, "I'm talking about Jesus of Nazareth, the One who hung on the cross just a few days ago." God's second arrow also hit Samuel, who was standing next to David. "This man who worked wonders and mighty miracles among you," Peter said, "you crucified Him! You killed Him. You nailed Him to the cross." The Holy Spirit drove the shaft home: "It was you, David. You killed Him too. It was you, Samuel. You killed Him too."

My friend, you already know that you helped kill Jesus too—with your sins. You are as guilty as David or Samuel were. Jesus was praying for you too when He said, "Father, forgive them; for they know not what they do." Peter's anointed words voided every excuse and left no one a place to hide. Then God pulled one more arrow from His quiver. The people had been hit, but they were not cut to the quick. By this time, Samuel was probably saying, "David, let's get out of here—*now!*"

If you are feeling the same way as you read these words, then you need to be careful. This may be your last opportunity. If you have a hardened heart, you will mistake the arrow of the Lord that was meant for good for something evil. God isn't out to simply "mess up your life" or spoil your little party; He wants to totally change your life and bless you. The arrows of the Lord have pierced you with conviction, and you can feel the power of the Word of God at this moment.

Peter continued to preach and the Lord aimed a third volley at young David and others of like heart. As God pulled out His third arrow, the people were already staggering. They felt the second stroke of God in their hearts when Peter said, "You nailed Him to the tree and killed Him. You crucified the Lord with your sins. You are responsible. You are guilty of murder." Suddenly, God again draws back His third arrow as Peter says, "You killed Him, but I have news for you: God raised Him from the dead!"

The arrow of the Lord exploded in a rush of deadly speed, and the crowd suddenly buckled over under the impact of that arrow. "There is hope? Wait a minute. I was the one beating my breast on Golgotha Hill, but now you say He is risen from the dead? What must I do? How can I get right with God?" Peter had hit the bull's eye. He said to himself, "This is what I have been waiting for!" Then he shouted to the shocked crowd, "Repent! Repent. Ask Jesus Christ to forgive you and wash your sins away. He will forgive you! Then you must be baptized in Jesus' name." Peter did not tell the people to "go home and think about it." No, he said, "Repent now!"

Repent. Go from an awakened heart to a believing heart. A believing heart is a broken and contrite heart that has been pierced through by the arrows of the Lord. The arrows of the Lord have been unleashed in these pages and they have pierced your heart whether you are a sinner or a saint. You can be like David and repent, or you can be like Samuel and harden your heart in cynical disbelief. You have been hit by the arrows of God just like my hypothetical characters, David, Elizabeth, and Ruthie. There is only one thing left to do: Repent.

> *O Lord, rebuke me not in Thy wrath: neither chasten me in Thy hot displeasure. For Thine arrows stick fast in me, and Thy hand presseth me sore. There is no soundness in my flesh because of Thine anger; neither is there any rest in my bones because of my sin. For mine iniquities are gone over mine head: as an heavy burden they are too heavy for me. My wounds stink and are corrupt because of my foolishness. I am troubled; I am bowed down greatly; I go mourning all the day long. For my loins are filled with a loathsome disease: and there is no soundness in my flesh. I am feeble and sore broken: I have roared by reason of the disquietness of my heart* (Psalm 38:1-8).

"I go mourning all the day long" (Ps. 38:6b). This describes the people I saw in my vision that morning, the people who went home with arrows sticking out of their bodies. Many of them were buckled over. Why? The arrows of the Lord had struck them. Arrows used for hunting and for war were barbed so they couldn't be pulled out without causing even more injury. If you are struck by an arrow of God, the best thing you can do is fall on your knees and allow the Holy Spirit to perform surgery on your soul. He's the only one who can remove those arrows. To be pricked or pierced by the arrow of the Lord is to be stung by the Lord until it draws blood.

I am going to give you an opportunity to repent and come to the Lord right now. On October 8, 1871, D.L. Moody preached to the largest congregation ever assembled in his tabernacle in Chicago. His text was Matthew 27:22: "What shall I do then with Jesus which is called Christ?" The people hung on every word, and Moody concluded by saying, "I want you to take this text home with you and turn it over in your minds during the next week. Next Sunday we will come to Calvary on the cross and we will decide what to do with Jesus of Nazareth." Ira Sankey stood up and sang, "Today the Savior calls, for refuge fly, the storm of justice falls and death is nigh," and they closed the service. That very night the great Chicago fire broke out, killing thousands and leaving the entire city in ashes. D.L. Moody to his dying day regretted his delay in calling the people to repentance right after that message. He later said, "I would rather have my right hand cut off than to give a congregation a week to decide what they will do with Jesus."

Friend, I'm not going to live my life with regret. I'm not going to give you a week. You're going to have to decide now. What about it, friend? Have the arrows of the Lord pierced your heart? Do you want to be forgiven? Three thousand people gave their lives to Jesus Christ after that first gospel sermon. Now it's your turn. Pray this prayer out loud right where you are:

Dear Jesus, thank You for piercing my heart with Your love. Thank You for taking my place on that cross and shedding Your blood for me. I can't wait one minute longer—I repent of my sins. I am sorry I wounded Your heart again. Please forgive me, wash my sins away, and make me new. Be my Savior and Lord, and my very best friend. I am Yours and You are mine. I give You my life, Lord Jesus. In Your precious name I pray. Amen.

End Note

1. James Strong, *The Comprehensive Concordance to the Bible* (Iowa Falls, IA: World Bible Publishers, n.d.), #2660: *katanusso*, kat-an-oos'-so; from G2596 and G3572; to pierce thoroughly, i.e. (fig.) to agitate violently ("sting to the quick"):—prick.

Chapter 12

The Violence of Revival

This revival is known in hell. I can hear the thundering hoofbeats of hell's legions of demons moving toward this mighty, world-shaking revival, even as believers from around the world call our offices to say, "All Heaven is breaking loose here since we have been to the revival in Pensacola!" Across the country, pastors who returned to their flocks after visiting the revival are sending back incredible reports. One pastor called from Iowa and said, "In the first week after we returned from the revival, we had two hundred conversions! Never in the history of our church have we seen anything like it."

I have also heard the agitated war cry of the enemy, not at a distance, but up close. Many fired-up believers are beginning to feel like they are involved in literal hand-to-hand combat with the hordes of hell. "Brother, I was delivered and I went through a season of victory, but now all hell is breaking loose in my life!" Why? When the enemy of your soul is fighting for survival, he will flood your mind with negative thoughts and ideas birthed in the red-hot canals of hell. You may feel like you are being let down into a cesspool of sinful thoughts just to see if you can pass the test of keeping your mind pure. There is a Christ, and I serve Him, but I also live in a real world that is full of demons and devils, not on some cloud somewhere. If you are any threat at all to the kingdom of darkness, then you should be going through something.

Let me put it another way: *You are not at war if everything is peaceful.* If you are reading the same Holy Bible I'm reading, then you realize that the peace and joy God gives us are supernatural so they will shine in the midst of bitter conflict and fighting with the dark realm. Paul's writings are filled with battlefield language. We are buffeted. We battle. We fight. We are taking on the strongholds of hell.

Forget the war games; this is war. I am not interested in manufactured crises or football rally hype as tools to "motivate" saints. I don't need these things when I'm talking to people who only three weeks before were snatched from the searing flames of hell and the torment of satan. Those people are *already* motivated! My problem is that I got spoiled in the Argentine revival. I watched "average" men of God simply stretch out their hands in faith and say, "Satan, in the name of Jesus I bind you!" When they waved their hands across a praying crowd of 10,000, people a half mile away would begin screaming out for deliverance. Demon-possessed people who were walking by the campaign site on their way to get an ice cream cone suddenly began to shake violently and fall into the street, spitting up and foaming at the mouth as they were mightily delivered from their demonic torment. There is power in unified shouts of war from God's people—especially when they are willing to pay a price in prayer and fasting for souls. When you get around some of those men, they ask you, "Does it not say, 'Greater is He who is in us...?' " Let's go to war! The first shots have been fired and the troops are moving in.

War is violent. Jesus Christ our Savior delivers us from the clutches of satan at an altar, in our homes, or on a street corner, but Jesus Christ our Lord leads us directly to God's recruiting station where we sign on the dotted line to join the Lord's army as a "lifer." He puts us on the next bus to boot camp. That is where we see our curly locks and snow-white Reeboks traded in for a head shave and spit-shined black combat boots. Our tennis shorts and "No fear" T-shirts are swapped for Holy Ghost camouflage fatigues. Mama's homemade biscuits, our nice colorful bedrooms, warm beds, and fluffy pillows, are left behind in exchange for "three hots [meals] and a cot." We're in the Army now—we wake up to reveille at 5:00 a.m., and strap on a 50-pound backpack for a 5-mile run.

However, no amount of training can prepare us for the violence of genuine war. I can tell you what it is going to be like out there fighting hell and casting out demons. I can tell you what it is like to be harvesting souls and to suddenly face 12 of satan's finest "black beret storm demons." The truth is that until you experience it for yourself, until you feel the heat of hell, until you feel the temptations rising in your life and the carnality rising in your own flesh, you won't under-stand the violence of revival. You have to hear the enemy whisper in your ear, "You're never going to make it! Look at what just went through your mind. Think about what you just looked at. You're not worthy." Until you experience the violence of revival for yourself, friend, then all the preach-ing, the lectures, and the Sunday school teaching just won't prepare you for it. You have to experience it for yourself.

You may be backslidden right now because you went to war and got hit hard by the enemy. Somebody dragged your wounded carcass into a revival service or put this book in your hands while you were still lying in a pool of blood. You've been hit hard and you saw things out there on the battlefield that made you think, *No one told me that Christian-ity could be so hard.* Perhaps you modeled yourself after some superstar and were disappointed. I like to model myself after people who have really fought hell and won. It was mostly a lot of "no-name Christians" who fought hell so we could live on American soil and be free to preach the gospel today. Many were decapitated, burned at the stake, fed to lions, and tortured for the name of Christ. They paid the price then for our religious freedom today. I owe it to Christ Jesus, to those who went before us, and to you to tell you the truth about the violence of revival.

This message has two points. Number one: *Your salvation was won by the violence of the cross.* The ministers of Christ should be violent too! I confess to you that I am a violent man and I am determined to snatch people out of hell's bondage! I'm going to go in and take them out no matter what it costs. If I see you suffering, I will snatch you out of the gates of hell. I'll do whatever it takes. You need to become violent when it comes to your salvation and the salvation of others. Why? Because your salvation was won by the violence of the cross.

Two thousand years ago Heaven's Commando stormed hell in an all-out attack. No longer was He going to accept bulls, rams, goats, sheep, turtledoves, and grain offerings. No longer was He going to look at the wickedness of men. Just before the invasion, before the birth of Christ, a deathly silence hovered over the land of men for four hundred long years. There were no holy prophets screaming warnings in the darkness. There were no street corner preachers pleading with the lost to get right with God. There was only silence and spiritual darkness.

To win your salvation, Jesus had to come and personally die a violent death in your place. He was bruised, crushed, punctured, whipped, ridiculed, spat upon, scorned, and abused for you and I. His gentle healing hands and holy feet were pierced just before He was subjected to the most violent death of His day: crucifixion on the cross of the condemned. He waged violent warfare for your salvation. He drank every bitter drop in His cup of suffering. He endured unendurable pain and violence for you.

God did not send an "associate" for this "sure death" mission; He sent His only Son. Your salvation was won through violence—and don't ever let anybody tell you differently. When He was hanging on that shameful cross in the nude before a mocking crowd of sinners, those scoffers were not whispering at Him. They were cursing and screaming at Him, "If You are *really* the Son of God, then get off that cross!" When He said, "It is finished," when His bloody head dropped and He died, there was a violent reaction! The earth quaked, the graves split open, the dead walked among the living, and the great woven veil in the temple was split in half from the top to the bottom by the infinite hand of God (see Mt. 27:51-53). All nature reeled at the death of the Lord Jesus Christ. Your salvation was won by a violent sacrifice at the crucifixion.

My second point is this: Since Jesus did His part, *you must wage violent warfare against sin.* If you want Jesus Christ to touch you and forgive you today, then you had better get violent about it. Get up and shake the devil off your lap. If you are sick of seeing sin waste away your life, then you must wage war. The violent man goes to war against his sins. Don't makes excuses; just get rid of them. Annihilate them with the sword of God's Word and burn them in God's fire without mercy. This is war. If you are struggling with pornography, don't let the devil fool you. Burn it. Destroy it. Wage war. The violent man takes the Kingdom of God by force.

Commit violent acts against your sin. If your neighbor sees you burning pornography and asks what you are doing, say, "I'm burning my *Penthouse* collection." If he says, "Hey, don't burn them—give them to me," you tell him, "Never in a million years. Watch them burn." That is violent. Don't strike a compromise and don't sign a treaty with sin. There is no room for negotiating or dealing with the devil. The Bible says to resist him and he will flee (see Jas. 4:7).

The salvation of your family and friends may depend *on you*! Wage violent warfare on their behalf. During the years I was in the Argentine revival, I saw the inner workings of the revival. The first place I took visiting pastors to was behind the scenes, underneath the platform that stood eight feet above the ground. As many as 300 prayer warriors were in a constant hum of prayer interrupted by violent roars of intercession in that space. This went on for eight hours throughout the meeting. If you stood on the platform, you could feel the floor literally rumble from the warlike intercession taking place underneath you! If you stood up and spoke by the Holy Ghost, "Lucifer, I come against you in the name of Jesus Christ," then you could feel the sheer power of that warfare tap into the command with stunning force.

Those warriors came to pray for hours and hours and hours—they were fighting for the Argentines and waging warfare on behalf of visitors who had flown in from India, Russia, Japan, and America to be prayed for. We do the same in Pensacola today—we wage violent no-quarter warfare in prayer. We plead the blood of the Lamb and the name of Jesus over everyone who comes to find more of God. We don't play games. There are souls on the line.

People are praying in Latin America as never before. All-night prayer vigils are held in homes, churches, and public places. They are powerful, loud, and insistent rallies attended many times by hundreds and thousands of people from all over a region. The Latin American church has learned there truly is power in prayer. Last year in Cali, Colombia, 40,000 Christians joined together and filled a stadium for a prayer rally—not for an evangelistic meeting or a Christian concert. That rally lasted into the wee hours of the night, and those people went to war in the spirit for their country, their cities, their churches, and their families. They confronted by name the principalities and powers that are strongholds in their regions, including the spirits related to the illegal drug traffic.

The powerful drug cartels in Colombia are on the run. I know the police do their best, but it is the warfare of fearless Christian prayer warriors that is winning the battle. Many believe that the pressure of fierce spiritual warfare instigated the assassination by drug lords of Pastor Julio Sanrubio on the front steps of a local church after the rally. He was one of the main organizers of this prayer rally. Nevertheless, prayer goes on. In Latin America, the people are used to the idea of literally giving their lives for what they stand for.

The Lord spoke to me and told me that many of you reading this book are "prisoners of war." If you have been taken captive by the enemy, then through the help of the Holy Ghost, we have broken through the camp and opened the door to your cell! We are going to jerk you out of that place and walk you right past the armed guards at the broken gates! You're coming all the way out today—but first you have to *want* to be set free.

Revival means violent upheaval and overthrow of principalities in the spirit realm. If you are afraid of warfare and violence, then it is too late. You have landed in the middle of a life-and-death battle. But you have everything you need for victory, so it's time for you to get on the front line of this war. Go after it. You are going to experience victories. Yes, you will feel the heat of hell as you get closer and closer to those flames, but a supernatural joy and strength will flood your soul as you begin to pull people out of hell's fires! This is why you were reborn into God's mighty Kingdom: You were ordained to be a violent soldier who delights in snatching the struggling, wounded, and dying prisoners of war right out of hell's fire and satan's grasp!

Emotionalism? No. This is real. I want to tell you something else too: We are winning. Hell shudders when this army rises to march. Now we can *really* sing, "Onward Christian soldiers, marching as to war." We are seeing it. Teenagers are walking into their schools with boldness, and they will bring thousands to Jesus each school year. They are militant, they hold their heads up, and they are absolutely unashamed of the gospel of the Lord Jesus Christ. They don't want anything to do with the old "shame-faced, head-bowed, embarrassed" brand of Christianity. This is violent warfare.

> *Verily I say unto you, Among them that are born of women there hath not risen a greater than John the Baptist: notwithstanding he that is least in the kingdom of heaven is greater than he. And from the days of John the Baptist until now the kingdom of heaven suffereth violence, and the violent take it by force* (Matthew 11:11-12).

The Amplified Bible says, "And from the days of John the Baptist until the present time, the kingdom of heaven has endured violent assault, and violent men seize it by force [as a precious prize…]" (Mt. 11:12). John the Baptist was an aggressive man of war. Forget the silly mental pictures of crickets and grasshoppers, and a character out of the "Flintstones" animated TV show. This wild man wore camel hair. He was an unwavering man of war who came for one reason and one reason only: to prepare the way of the Lord. His face was set like a flint. When Herod's rage was leveled toward him, he stood his ground; but when people applauded him, he shook off man's praise and adoration. He was a man on a mission who was dead to the world and alive to God. He didn't wear fashionable clothes or dine at the banqueting tables of kings and queens. He waged warfare in the wilderness, and every sermon carried one essential violent theme: repent.

My friend, *repent* is the most violent word in the Bible! John called sin "sin." Hypocrisy was hypocrisy. Dead religion was dead religion, no matter whose name was attached to it. He told the people who came to be baptized, "You brood of vipers. Who warned you to flee from the wrath to come?" and "The ax is already laid at the root of the tree. Every tree that does not bear good fruit is cut down and thrown into the fire. Amen. Now I baptize you...." Then he said, "I baptize you with water, but there is somebody coming after me who is going to baptize you in fire..." (see Mt. 3:7-11). Can you imagine what those people thought? Baptism is immersion, and fire is hot!

Pastors, John the Baptist told the Jews the ugly truth and they flocked to him in repentance. America knows where it stands—don't try to lie to Americans. You can tell them God loves them all day long, but they want to hear about judgment. They want to know the truthful answer to the question, "Am I going to make it to Heaven?" You need to tell them, "You're going to go to hell in your sin if you don't repent and ask Jesus for mercy!" The people in John's day had seen all the religious hypocrisy. They had heard all of the "pillow prophets" lulling them to sleep with religious sweet nothings. Then they heard hard-preaching John the Baptist say, "You brood of vipers, you have come to be baptized, but if you don't start bearing good fruit for the Kingdom of God, the ax is already laid to the root! The Messiah will chop you down and cut you to ribbons." So why did they follow such a no-nonsense, "narrow-minded" preacher? The hearts of the people bore witness to the truth!

Teenagers are flocking to this revival by the thousands. Why? They know this is the truth. And that is why hundreds of seasoned church pastors and ordained ministers publicly wept and cried at the front of a recent ministers' convention. I could have talked to them all day long about the anointing, revival, or church growth, but God told me to preach about *sin*—they knew they were walking in sin, and God will not bless it! They desperately wanted the charade to be over, and once their sin was exposed, they ran to the altar to repent and be free. Tell people the truth—no matter what the consequence.

John the Baptist was a violent aggressor and an irritant to the religious leaders of his day. He was a rough, tough, military man clothed in the Lord's battle fatigues. He was a prophet's prophet who wielded the two-edged sword of the Lord like a skilled Green Beret or Navy SEAL. He sliced through demon-inspired doctrines and mutilated mediocrity. He was a violent, God-fearing man on a violent mission of revival.

Two thousand years ago, Heaven stormed hell in an all-out attack and won. Jesus waged violent warfare to save the entire race of imprisoned mankind. So today, we say "America loves God." For some superstitious reason, we think God is watching over and blessing this country. "After all," we say, "everybody loves God. Americans go to church two or three times a year. We love God. Even our money says, 'In God we trust.'" Garbage, friend. Any man, woman, or child who truly appreciates what the Lord Jesus Christ did will give their life to Him without conditions, limitations, or hesitation. If you are a backslider, friend, then you had better understand that every time you sin, you are driving those rough iron nails deeper into His holy wrists and ankles. You might as well be holding that whip yourself and raking it across His back as you turn His body into ribbons of mutilated flesh. Every time you sin, you crucify Him again! Stop your sin.

The physical pain of Calvary, as bad as it was, ended about 2,000 years ago, but the true pain of Calvary endures to this day. When you know that He died for you and yet live in a realm of denial, Jesus feels the pain of rejection anew. He aches when He watches you sin over and over again and spit in the face of your heavenly Father who loves you so much. That is the true pain of Calvary. When you choose to sin, you are once again beating the Lord's noble head and whipping His scarred back. Each mumbled excuse and spoken rejection reverberates as yet another curse on His name—and all along you know that He died for you on Calvary.

Millions of Americans remember the old hymns, but they will go to hell if someone doesn't step into the gap. That is why judgment must be preached alongside the truths of grace, mercy, and love. Sermons on Heaven are most powerful when accompanied by biblical sermons on hell. Don't worry about "convincing" your hearers; the Holy Ghost will do that through conviction! Don't be discouraged if you see heads drop—they haven't fallen asleep; they've fallen under the conviction! They will listen. Those church leaders at that ministers' convention responded immediately to the Holy Spirit. The truth transformed them into warriors who wanted to win a battle. They jumped up and raced to the altar. They were violent! They reclaimed their families by force! They asked for forgiveness for their sin, retrieved what the enemy had stolen, and waged war.

Jesus got violent about your salvation. Isn't it time for you to get violent about it too? Force your way through the jungles of hell and the muck and mire of evil thoughts. Crawl right over that cesspool of sin. God is going to heal and deliver you, but you have to get violent about it and take it by force! Get violent about the Kingdom of God and people will suddenly begin to see Jesus in your life. Heaven will look down and hell will look up and see that you are finally serious. This is war! Never look for peace while you proclaim war. Determine in your heart to be the victor!

Destiny Image
New Releases

ARROWS OF THE LORD *by Stephen Hill.*
How does God's Spirit work on the heart? God has a bow, and He has arrows. His arrows are sharp, strike like lightning, and stick fast. He is also a perfect shot. He knows where you are, and how to prepare the message for your heart and your heart for His message.
Videotape ISBN 1-56043-680-8 Retail $19.99

WHITE CANE RELIGION *by Stephen Hill.*
We are in the midst of an incredible, worldwide outpouring of the Holy Spirit. It is a day when everyone is following someone. It is vitally important that we take a look at who we are following. Do they know where *they* are going? "*If the blind lead the blind, both shall fall into the ditch*" (Mt. 15:14b).
Videotape ISBN 0-7684-0046-5 Retail $19.99

WHEN THE GAVEL FALLS *by Stephen Hill.*
There is coming a time when we will all stand before God. It is an appointment everyone will keep and no man can break. The only way to prepare for that time *up there* is to receive pardon *down here.* Yes, God has a legal system. We will all be summoned. There will be a trial and a verdict. Now is the time to prepare for when the gavel falls. Once it does fall...the case will be closed *forever.*
Videotape ISBN 0-7684-0044-9 Retail $19.99

THE POWER OF BROKENNESS
by Don Nori.
Brokenness—the disdain of tyrants and the wonder of kings. In this book you'll meet this companion who never forgets her need of mercy, never forgets the grace that flows on her behalf. She is the secret to knowing God's plans and desires, to obeying the Master's bidding, and to finding your way to your personal destiny.
Paperback Book, 168p. ISBN 1-56043-178-4 Retail $8.99

Available at your local Christian bookstore.

Internet: http://www.reapernet.com

Prices subject to change without notice.